Exam Skills Practice

Edexcel GCSE
Business

Extend

Student Workbook

Keith Hirst and Jonathan Shields

T0350581

PEARSON

Published by Pearson Education Limited, a company incorporated in England and Wales, having its registered office at Edinburgh Gate, Harlow, Essex, CM20 2JE. Registered company number: 872828
www.Pearsonschoolsandfecolleges.co.uk

Edexcel is a registered trademark of Edexcel Limited
Text © Pearson Education Limited 2011

First published 2011
ARP impression 98

British Library Cataloguing in Publication Data

A catalogue record for this book is available from the British Library
ISBN 978 1 446900 51 2

Typeset by Juice Creative
Cover design by Pearson Education Limited

Printed and bound in Great Britain by Ashford Colour Press Ltd

Disclaimer
The material has been published on behalf of Edexcel and offers high-quality support for the delivery of Edexcel qualifications. This does not mean that this material is essential to achieve any Edexcel qualification, nor does it mean that this is the only suitable material available to support any Edexcel qualification. Edexcel material will not be used verbatim in setting any Edexcel examination or assessment. Any resource lists produced by Edexcel shall include this and other appropriate resources. Copies of official specifications for all Edexcel qualifications may be found on the Edexcel website: www.edexcel.com.

Contents

About this book

This workbook has been written to help you practise your exam skills as you prepare for your GCSE Business Studies exam for either Unit 3 (Building a business) or Unit 5 (Introduction to economic understanding). You'll find practice activities for each question type you will face, helping you to demonstrate what you have learnt. You'll find answers to the activities at the back of the book, so that you can check whether you're on track after you've completed the activities.

What to expect in the exam paper

The assessment for Units 3 and 5 is through an examination worth 90 marks. You have one and a half hours for this examination. The examination is divided into three sections which include a variety of question types, including multiple choice, short answer questions and extended response questions.

In this workbook, the Unit 3 and Unit 5 questions and activities have been colour-coded to help you quickly find the ones relevant to you. The Unit 3 pages are blue and Unit 5 pages are orange.

There are three sections on Unit 3 and Unit 5 exam papers, and you must answer all questions in all three sections. Below is a summary of the different types of questions you can expect, and the pages in this book where information and activities can be found.

Summary of question types

Question type	Number of marks	Pages	I am confident with this ✓ / X
Objective test (multiple choice)	1 mark	6–8	
'Give', 'State' and 'Identify'	1–3 marks	9–11	
'What is meant by the term…?'	2 marks	12–14	
Questions using diagrams	1–4 marks	15–19	
'Calculate'	1–3 marks	20–24	
'Outline'	2–3 marks	25–31	
'Describe'	3–4 marks	32–38	
'Explain'	3 marks	39–45	
Choice	6 or 8 marks	46–54	
'Discuss'	6 or 8 marks	55–63	
'Assess'	8 or 10 marks	64–75	
'Using your knowledge of business/ economics, assess…'	10 marks	76–87	

How to use this book

This workbook has been planned to help you to build better answers. Activities have been designed to enable you to build the skills that will help you to achieve: understanding the exam question, using the mark scheme, building an answer, writing under timed conditions, and improving existing answers.

For many of the activities you will write into the book itself. Space is provided to allow you to do this.

 Where you see this symbol you need to use a separate sheet of paper for the activity.

Where you see boxes like these, take note! They are there to help you or remind you of important information.

Introduction to objective test questions

Objective test questions feature in **Section A**. Each paper will usually have four such questions.

Objective test questions will be multiple choice. For each question you are given four possible answers. One of these is correct. Beware though. The wrong options – the **distracters** – have been chosen to appear as though they could be correct. Even if you think you know the right answer, read the other options as well.

A student aiming for the top grades should try to correctly answer **all four** objective test questions.

A typical question

Business finance can come from either internal or external sources.

Which of the following is an internal source of finance? (1 mark)

*Select **one** answer.*

      A *A loan from a bank.*

      B *An overdraft.*

      C *Selling assets.*

      D *Selling shares.*

Strategies for getting the right answer

The following process can be used to help you when you are working through questions.

- **Highlight** the key terms in the question. The question above refers to **internal** sources of finance. This can be easily confused with **external** sources.

- **Read** all the options carefully.

- **Rule out** those you know are wrong. For example, you may know that Option A – a loan from a bank – is wrong as this is an **external** source of finance. You might also know that Option B – an overdraft – is similar to a loan and is therefore also an external source of finance.

- **Select** what you think is the right answer. As a business owns assets, selling them will raise finance. This finance comes from within the business and therefore C is the correct answer.

- **Check** D as well to ensure you are right. Selling shares is an **external** source of finance, so C is the correct answer.

> **Hint**
>
> Objective test questions generally test your knowledge of key terms. Make sure you actively learn your key terms as you are going through the course.

> **Remember**
>
> Don't dive in! Think about each option before you make your decision.

Activity 1: Understanding the exam question

Objective test questions are primarily designed to test knowledge and understanding. One important strategy you can use is to make sure you can spot **distracters**.

Identify in the table below which of the options are 'good' distracters – those that sound as though they might be accurate but are not – and those that are 'bad' distracters – those that are obviously wrong.

One of the options listed below is the correct answer. When you have found it, place a tick next to it in the answer column.

> **Hint**
>
> Distracters are those options which are incorrect. They are phrased in such a way to make you **think** rather than being very obviously wrong.

The encouragement of repeat purchase ensures that products will be sold on a regular basis. Repeat purchase is important because it…   *(1 mark)*

Option		Distracters		Answer
		Good	Bad	
A	…helps develop word of mouth advertising.			
B	…will help in the negotiation for lower priced raw materials.			
C	…will always reduce a business' costs.			
D	…helps to improve the business' customer service.			
E	…allows a business to develop brand loyalty amongst its customers.			
F	…involves re-training the sales force.			

Activity 2: Build an answer

Write a correct answer plus three possible distracters for the question below. Highlight which one is the correct answer by placing a tick next to it in the answer column.

*Which of the following best describes the term '**salary**'?*   *(1 mark)*

Distracter/Correct answer	Answer
A	
B	
C	
D	

Activity 1: Understanding the exam question

Objective test questions are primarily designed to test knowledge and understanding. One important strategy you can use is to make sure you can spot **distracters**.

Identify in the table below which of the options are 'good' distracters – those that sound as though they might be accurate but are not – and those that are 'bad' distracters – those that are obviously wrong.

One of the options listed below is the correct answer. When you have found it, place a tick next to it in the answer column.

Hint

Distracters are those options which are incorrect. These are phrased in such a way to make you **think**, rather than being very obviously wrong.

International trade is where countries import and export products.
Which of the following best describes an '**export**'?   (1 mark)

Option		Distracters		Answer
		Good	Bad	
A	A cost that a business needs to pay each month.			
B	A product made in another country.			
C	A tax imposed on products bought from foreign countries.			
D	An organisation which aims to influence business decisions.			
E	A product made in the UK and bought by a consumer in another country.			
F	Products only available in the UK.			

Activity 2: Build an answer

Write a correct answer plus three possible distracters for the question below. Highlight which one is the correct answer by placing a tick next to it in the answer column.

Which of the following best describes '**economies of scale**'?   (1 mark)

Distracter/Correct answer	Answer
A	
B	
C	
D	

Introduction to 'Give', 'State' and 'Identify' questions

'Give', 'State' and 'Identify' questions will usually be found in **Section A** of the exam paper. Some will also appear in Sections B and C.

To answer this kind of question you need to write a simple list of points using one or two words, a simple phrase or a short sentence. Each different and correct point you make is worth **one mark**.

A student aiming for the top grades should try to correctly answer all of these questions.

> **Hint**
>
> You do **not** need to write a lengthy sentence for each point you make. Usually one or two words or a simple phrase will be enough.

How will I be marked?

You will gain 1 mark for each different and correct point that you make.

A typical question

*Identify **two** methods Amazon might use to differentiate its service from its rivals. (2 marks)*

A 2-mark answer

Larger range of products.

Fast delivery.

Why does this answer gain 2 marks?

Two points are made and both points are different.

> **Hint**
>
> In questions like this, make sure that your two points are different enough. If you wrote:
>
> 1. New products.
>
> 2. Bigger range of products.
>
> … you might only get 1 mark, because the two points you have made are too similar.

Activity 1: Using the mark scheme

Look at the question below:

> Identify **two** methods of 'product trial' that Subway could use.   *(2 marks)*

Now look at the mark scheme for this question:

> Award 1 mark for each appropriate response.
>
> Do not award a mark for very similar answers, e.g. advertising on ITV and advertising on Sky.

1. Use the mark scheme to mark Student A's answer below. Place your mark in the box below the answer.

Student A:

1. Subway could do lots of advertising, this will encourage lots of people to try its sandwiches for the first time and come to its shops.

2. Subway could offer money-off vouchers. This will make its sandwiches better value for money, meaning that more people will try them compared to other sandwich shops like Pret A Manger.

Mark awarded =   /2

2. Now use a highlighter pen to highlight exactly which parts of the answer scored the marks. Try to highlight as few words as possible that will allow this answer to score the same marks.

Students who are aiming for the top grades often feel that they have to write lots for these questions. This is not the case. You can write a short answer and this will give you more time for the longer questions. It is these longer questions that often make the difference between the top two grades.

3. Use the mark scheme to mark Student B's answer, again placing your mark in the box below:

Student B:

1. Offer free samples.

2. Low trial prices.

Mark awarded =   /2

Activity 1: Using the mark scheme

Look at the question below:

> *Identify **two** reasons why a business might want to grow.*   *(2 marks)*

Now look at the mark scheme for this question:

> Award 1 mark for each relevant reason:
>
> - To increase profits.
> - To increase market share.
> - To take advantage of economies of scale.
> - To gain more market power.
>
> Do not award a mark for very similar answers, e.g. 'higher profit' and 'to make more money'.

1. Use the mark scheme to mark Student A's answer below. Place your mark in the box below the answer.

Student A:

1. Businesses grow for many reasons. One important reason is that it might involve the business making more money (profit).

2. Another reason why a business may want to grow is to increase market share. This will mean that the business is able to charge higher prices as it has more market power over its competitors.

Mark awarded = [/2   ]

2. Now use a highlighter pen to highlight exactly which parts of the answer scored the marks. Try to highlight as few words as possible that will allow this answer to score the same marks.

Students who are aiming for the top grades often feel that they have to write lots for these questions. This is not the case. You can write a few words and this will give you more time for the longer questions. It is these longer questions that often make the difference between the top two grades.

3. Use the mark scheme to mark Student B's answer, again placing your mark in the box below:

Student B:

1. Economies of scale.

2. Increased revenue.

Mark awarded = [/2   ]

Introduction to 'What is meant by the term' questions

'What is meant by the term…' questions will usually be found in **Sections B and C** of the exam paper, but can sometimes be found in Section A.

To answer these questions you will need to provide a clear definition of the term. Since the question is worth 2 marks, there will usually be two elements to the definition which must be present in your answer.

A student aiming for the top grades should try to correctly answer all these questions.

A typical question

*What is meant by the term '**pressure group**'? (2 marks)*

A 2-mark answer

Pressure groups are organisations of people which seek to influence the decision-making of a firm or government.

Why does this answer gain 2 marks?

There is a clear understanding of what a pressure group is.

The answer contains two facts: pressure groups are 'organisations of people' and they are 'seeking to influence the decision-making of a firm or government'.

Remember
Even if you have not learnt the exact definition, try to extend your understanding of the term by writing an extra sentence or by giving an example.

For example, Greenpeace is a pressure group. Its members care about the environment and try to get the government to pass laws to reduce pollution.

Activity 1: Build an answer

Look at the question below:

> *What is meant by the term '**ethics**'?* *(2 marks)*

Now look at the mark scheme for this question:

> Two marks are given for an accurate definition. If an accurate definition is not given, award 1 mark for reference to the term 'morals' or implying a sense of 'right'.
>
> Developing the answer to indicate what this means can raise the answer to 2 marks. This could take the form of an additional clarifying sentence or example.

It is best to learn all the definitions of key terms in the specification. However, what if you panic and cannot remember the precise definition? Can you still get 2 marks from the mark scheme?

Look at Student A's answer below. Using the mark scheme, what mark would this answer score? Place your mark in the box below.

Student A:

Ethics is when a company does the right thing.

Mark awarded = [/2]

Now try to improve the answer by writing an additional sentence or example in the space below:

....

....

....

....

....

....

....

....

....

....

Remember
If you have not learnt an accurate definition, you can still write an imperfect definition and add an extra clarifying sentence or an example.

Activity 1: Build an answer

Look at the question below:

*What is meant by the term '**exchange rate**'?*   *(2 marks)*

Now look at the mark scheme for this question:

The market price at which one currency is sold in order to buy/exchange another currency.

Award 2 marks for a definition that includes reference to both price and exchange/expression related to another currency.

For 1 mark a limited definition is given such as 'The price of a currency' or '£1 = $1.60'. An imperfect definition can be raised to 2 marks through an extra clarifying sentence.

It is best to learn all the definitions of key terms in the specification. However, what if you panic and cannot remember the exact definition? Can you still get 2 marks for this kind of question?

Look at Student A's answer below. Using the mark scheme, what mark would this answer score? Place your mark in the box below.

Student A:

The exchange rate is how much a currency is worth.

Mark awarded = [/2]

Now try to improve the answer by writing an additional sentence or example in the space below:

....

....

....

....

....

....

....

....

....

Remember

If you have not learnt an accurate definition, you can still write an imperfect definition and add an extra clarifying sentence or an example.

Introduction to questions using diagrams

Some questions will require you to use a diagram. These questions are based on information contained in the diagram. They can appear in **Sections A, B or C**. Some diagrams require specific answers from the data. Others provide information on which to base an extended answer on.

Examples of the type of diagrams you may be required to use are:

○ break-even chart – Unit 3

○ stock control – Unit 3

○ product life cycle – Unit 3

○ economic growth – Unit 5

A student aiming for the top grades should try to score full marks on all questions using diagrams.

A typical question

Jason and Balvir have decided to use break-even analysis as part of the planning for their business. They are planning to offer a set menu for a price of £30.

Projected break-even - per month

Using the graph above, how many customers do Jason and Balvir need to break even each month? (1 mark)

Strategies for getting the right answer

○ **Thinking time:** Study the information carefully before you begin to answer.

○ **Axes:** Make sure you understand what the axes show. Highlight the labels if necessary.

○ **Write onto the diagram** if you think this will help. In the diagram above, the student has circled in blue where they think the break-even point is. This might help you to work out the answer.

○ **Units:** Make sure you provide the correct units with any answer you provide.

Break-even occurs where total revenue is equal to total costs. In this example, this point is at 500 customers.

Activity 1: Understanding the exam question

Tavistock Toy Chest is a small independent toy retailer.

The diagram below illustrates a bar gate stock chart for paddling pools at Tavistock Toy Chest.

Use the diagram below to answer the following questions:

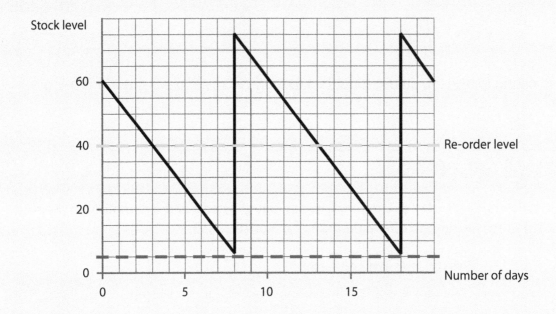

1. Calculate how many paddling pools the business holds as a buffer stock. (1 mark)

....

2. Calculate the number of paddling pools that arrived on day 8. Show your workings. (2 marks)

....

....

....

3. Calculate how many days it will take for the order of paddling pools to arrive at the business after re-ordering. (2 marks)

....

....

....

On the diagram above draw a coloured line showing how you worked out the answer to each question. Use a different coloured pen for each one.

Look at the questions below:

> Rattans Ltd is a business which makes and sells metal holiday souvenirs.
>
> **Question 1:** Last month Rattans Ltd sold 1000 souvenirs.
> Use the diagram below to calculate its margin of safety.
> Show your workings. *(2 marks)*
>
> **Question 2:** Use the diagram to calculate the loss Rattans Ltd would
> make if they only made and sold 500 souvenirs per month.
> Show your workings. *(2 marks)*

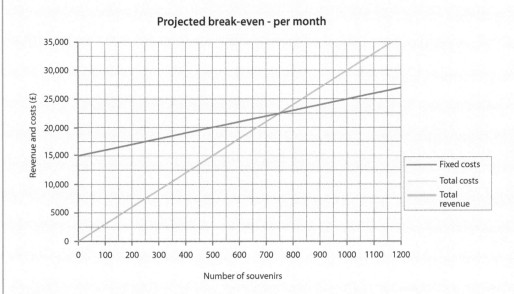

When answering diagram questions, the most important thing to remember is that all of the information you need is on the diagram.

To answer question 1, you need to:

○ find the break-even level of output

○ then subtract this figure from Rattans' current output (stated in the question)

○ remember to show evidence of workings in your answer, otherwise you will not get all of the marks.

To answer question 2, you need to:

○ draw a vertical line up at 500 units, reading off the figures for total revenue and total costs

○ put these figures into the formula for profit and calculate the answer

○ remember to show evidence of workings in your answer, otherwise you will not get all of the marks.

 On a separate piece of paper, use the diagram to answer both of the questions. You or a friend can then mark the answers using the mark scheme on page 92.

Remember
Do not give yourself more than 2 minutes for each question.

Activity I: Understanding the exam question

If a question provides a diagram, you should spend some time making sense of the information it contains. You will then be able to use this information in the questions that follow.

> The diagram below shows UK inflation from 2007–2009. Study this data and identify **two** trends in the data. Provide reasons for the trends.
>
> An example is provided for you in the table below.   *(2 marks)*

UK inflation (Consumer Prices Index)

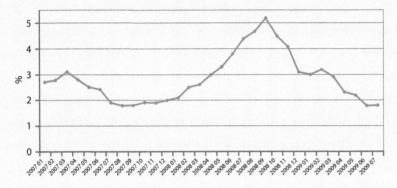

In 2009 many families felt the benefits of lower inflation. Inflation, as measured by the Consumer Prices Index (CPI), was 5.2% in September 2008, largely due to rising gas, electricity and food prices.

By September 2009 the CPI was 1.6%. One of the main reasons for the slowdown in inflation was a fall in the prices of basic items.

> **Hint**
>
> Look for where the biggest changes take place.

Answer the question in the table below.

Dates	Trend identified	Possible reasons
2007(3)–2007(8)	Inflation slows from 3% to just under 2%.	Less spending in the economy, possibly due to rising unemployment. People have less disposable income.

Activity 2: Understanding the exam question

Some questions will ask you to 'use an example' from the diagram.

Look at the question below:

> *The diagram below shows the exchange rate of the pound against the dollar from 2000–2007. Using an example from the graph, state what is meant by a 'strong pound'.*
>
> *(2 marks)*

Exchange rate $ (US dollars) per £ (UK pound)

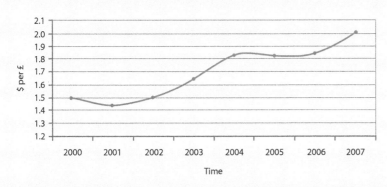

Hint

The question asks you to 'use an example'.

Look at the three student responses below and award each a mark.
Give reasons to support your decision.

Response		Mark	Reason
A	A strong pound is where the pound grows in value.		
B	Where the pound will buy more dollars than it used to. For example, in 2001 £1 would buy $1.45 but in 2007 it would buy $2.00.		
C	Where the pound strengthens against foreign currencies. It means UK consumers get more dollars for every pound they spend. This is good for UK consumers as goods and services from the US become cheaper.		

Introduction to 'Calculate' questions

'Calculate' questions will usually be found in **Section B** of the exam paper.

'Calculate' questions involve using numbers and a formula. To answer 'Calculate' questions you will need to state the formula you are using, then show your workings by placing the correct numbers into the formula. This should then be followed by an answer stated in the correct units. A calculator will be useful in making sure you answer the question correctly.

A student aiming for the top grades should try to score full marks on all 'Calculate' questions.

Hint

There are very few mathematical formulae that you will need for the exam. In Unit 3 you need to know the formulae for the break-even point, the margin of safety and profit. You will also need to understand how a bar gate stock graph works. In Unit 5 you will need to be able to calculate the effect of changing exchange rates.

A typical question

Sony's fixed costs for the PlayStation® 3 are £2,400,000 and variable costs are £140 per console.

Calculate the break-even point when the PlayStation® 3 was priced at £300. Show your workings and the formula used. (3 marks)

A 3-mark answer

$$\text{Break-even} = \frac{\text{Total Fixed Costs}}{\text{Price} - \text{AVC}}$$

Therefore:

$$\text{Break-even} = \frac{£2,400,000}{(£300 - £140)}$$

Break-even = 15,000 consoles.

Why does this response gain 3 marks?

The question asks you to state the formula and show your workings. This means that 1 mark is awarded for doing each of these things. The final mark is awarded for the answer.

Remember

These questions are generally easy and are not designed to trick you. You need to learn your formulae to have any chance of getting these questions right. Make a list of the key formulae you will need as part of your revision notes and make sure you learn them accurately.

Activity 1: Using the mark scheme

Look at the question below:

Jason and Balvir have decided to use break-even analysis as part of the planning for their new restaurant. They are planning to offer a set menu for a price of £30. They have estimated their costs as:

- *Fixed costs = £8000*

- *Variable costs are £14 per set menu*

Calculate the break-even point. Give the formula and show your workings. (3 marks)

Now look at the mark scheme for this question:

1 mark for the identification of the formula, 1 mark for demonstrating workings and 1 mark for the correct answer.

$$\text{Break-even} = \frac{\text{Total Fixed Costs}}{(\text{Price} - \text{AVC})} \qquad \text{Break-even} = \frac{£8000}{(£30 - £14)}$$

Break-even = 500 meals.

Use the mark scheme to mark the answer below. Place your mark in the box below the answer.

Student A:

Contribution per unit = £30 – £14 = £16

Total fixed costs = £8000

Therefore break-even occurs at 500 meals.

Mark awarded = [/3]

Explain in the space below how this answer could be improved to score full marks:

....

....

....

....

....

....

....

....

Activity 2: Build an answer

Look at the question below:

Sony's fixed costs for the PlayStation® 3 are £2,400,000 and variable costs are £140 per console.

Calculate the level of profit or loss Sony would have made if it had sold 20,000 PlayStation® 3 consoles at £300. Show your workings and the formula used. (3 marks)

Now look at the mark scheme for this question:

1 mark for the identification of the formula, 1 mark for demonstrating workings and 1 mark for the correct answer.

Use the diagram below to help you answer the question. The process is shown on the left. Answer the question by filling in the boxes on the right, so that you demonstrate three separate stages.

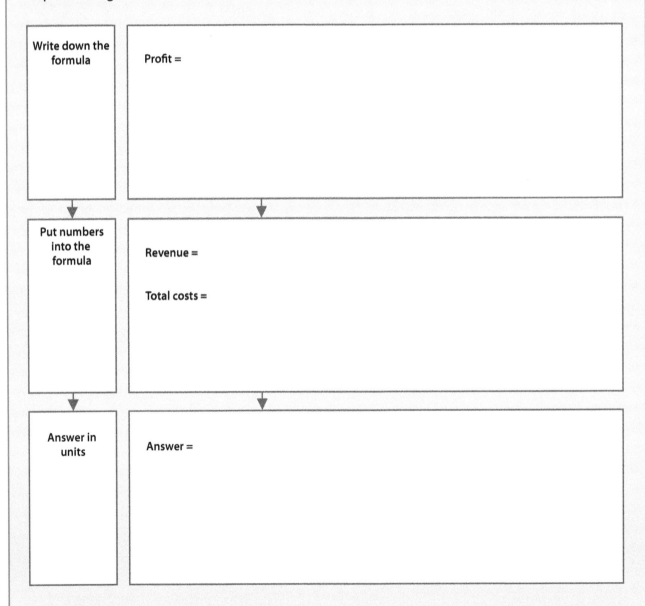

Write down the formula	Profit =
Put numbers into the formula	Revenue = Total costs =
Answer in units	Answer =

If you follow this simple three-stage approach to answering 'Calculate' questions, you should gain top marks (providing your arithmetic is sound and you have learnt the formulae).

Activity 1: Build an answer

Note: 'Calculate' questions are **not** usually a feature of Unit 5. However, you do need to understand some numerical measurements. Specifically:

- price sensitivity
- productivity
- exchange rates
- total revenue
- total costs
- profit

Look at the question below:

A football club charges an average of £20 per ticket. For a typical game the club has an attendance of 10,000. The club decides to increase its price to £25. Attendance at a typical game falls to 9000.

Use the idea of price sensitivity to suggest the most appropriate price for this business, if its objective was to increase revenue.　　　　*(3 marks)*

To answer this question you first need to work out how much revenue the business has for each price:

Price = £20	Price = £25
Attendance = 10,000	Attendance = 9000
Total revenue = 20 x 10,000 = £200,000	Total revenue = £25 x 9000 = £225,000

So – revenue has increased as a result of this business increasing its price. Interesting. Note that the question asks you to 'Use the idea of price sensitivity...' In the space below, briefly outline which price the business should use. Make sure you use your calculations in your answer:

....

....

....

....

....

....

....

....

Activity 2: Build an answer

Look at the question below:

> *Charles Mitchell imports high quality pasta from Northern Italy for sale at his delicatessen in Suffolk. The exchange rate between the pound (£) and the euro (€) is important for Charles. He buys 100 kg of pasta every month. The price of pasta is €5 per kg.*
>
> *In April, the exchange rate is £1.00 = €1.25. Calculate how much Charles has to pay to buy his pasta in this month.*
> *(3 marks)*

Now look at the mark scheme for this question:

> 1 mark for the identification of the formula, 1 mark for demonstrating workings and 1 mark for the correct answer.

Remember

To convert from euro to pounds you need to divide by the exchange rate. If you need to convert from pounds to euro, you multiply by the exchange rate.

Use the diagram below to help you answer the question. The process is given on the left. Answer the question by filling in the boxes on the right, so that you demonstrate three separate stages. The first box has been started for you.

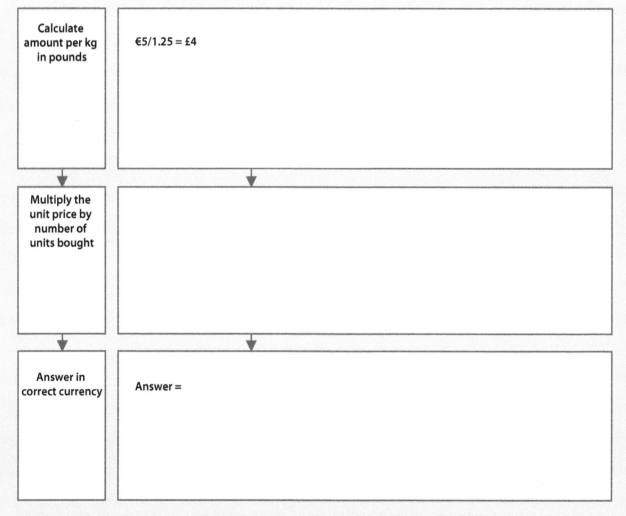

Calculate amount per kg in pounds	€5/1.25 = £4
Multiply the unit price by number of units bought	
Answer in correct currency	Answer =

If you follow this simple three-stage approach to answering 'Calculate' questions, you should gain top marks (providing your arithmetic is sound and you have learnt the formulae).

Introduction to 'Outline' questions

'Outline' questions will be found mostly in **Sections A and B** of the exam paper, but also possibly in Section C. These can be worth 2 or 3 marks.

To answer an 'Outline' question you need to take note of the number of marks available. When dealing with these questions you can make a number of points using sentences. These may be linked. In a 2-mark question you might make one point and develop it and, in a 3-mark question, you should make up to two points with one developed.

Where a question asks you to outline **one** factor or method, for example, the points you make should link to the factor or method you have identified. If you provide a list of points with no development you will only score 1 mark.

A student aiming for the top grades should try to gain full marks on this type of question.

> **Hint**
> It is a good idea to use an example to 'outline' a factor or method.

A typical question

*Outline **one** method a business might use to increase its profit. (2 marks)*

A 2-mark answer

Profits could be increased by cutting costs. If revenue stays the same, profits will rise.

Why does this answer gain 2 marks?

The point is made that 'cutting costs' will help to increase profits – this is the method. This scores 1 mark. A further mark is awarded for the development, which shows understanding of the relationship between costs, revenue and profit.

> **Hint**
> Careful! Using the word 'also' implies a second method. The question doesn't ask for this.

A 1-mark answer

Profits could be increased by selling more products. Also, the business could cut its costs.

Why does this answer only gain 1 mark?

The method given is 'selling more products' – this would gain 1 mark. The last sentence is a separate point. The question asks for **one** method only.

> **Remember**
> If the question is worth 2 marks, you should make one point and develop it.

Activity 1: Using the mark scheme

Look at the question below:

*Outline **one** consumer protection law that Marks & Spencer must follow.*   *(2 marks)*

Now look at the mark scheme below:

1 mark for the identification of one consumer protection law, and one mark for some kind of development or example using the Marks & Spencer context.

Mark the two student responses to the question above. There are 2 marks available for each question.

Hint

To answer an 'Outline' question worth 2 marks you should make one point and give some development using sentences. These may be linked.

Student A:

Sale of Goods Act.

Trades Description Act.

Mark awarded	Reasons

Student B:

Marks & Spencer must make sure that they follow the Trades Description Act. This means when they say on the label that a shirt is made out of cotton, it cannot be made out of nylon instead.

Mark awarded	Reasons

Activity 2: Understanding the question

Read the following question. Then look at the different student responses in the table below.

*Outline **any** problems a business might face by having too much stock.* (3 marks)

Decide whether the student responses in the table below provide statements that are developed. If they do, place a tick in the second column. If they do not, put a cross in the second column.

In both cases, use the third column to explain the reasons behind your decision.

Response		Developed?	Reasons
A	By having too much stock you will need a bigger warehouse to store it in. Buying lots of stock also means you also have to spend lots of money buying it.		
B	By having too much stock you will need to have a bigger warehouse to store it in. This will mean that the business will face extra costs which will reduce its profits.		
C	By having too much stock you will increase your costs. You will also increase the amount of space you need to store the stock. All of the extra stock will also need to be insured in case the warehouse burns down.		

Activity 3: Improve an answer

Look at the question below:

> Outline **one** way in which a stronger brand name could benefit a business.　　　(2 marks)

Think about how each of the two student answers below might be improved. The tables suggest possible improvements for each answer. Indicate with a tick or a cross in the second column whether each suggestion will improve the answer. In the right hand column offer reasons to support your decision.

Student A:

A strong brand name means that the business will be able to sell more of its products. It also means that it will be able to sell its products for a higher price. This is because people who see the branding will like it and want to be associated with it.

	Suggested improvement	Does this help?	Reasons
A	Provide definitions of terms.		
B	Link together different parts of the answer.		
C	Use paragraphs to organise the answer.		
D	Provide lots of detail, as many concepts as possible.		
E	Provide one point and develop it.		

Student B:

A strong brand will benefit a business because it will increase its profits. This is because a strong brand makes the product more attractive to the consumer. This then means that the consumer will pay a higher price for each product that they buy.

	Suggested improvement	Does this help?	Reasons
A	Link together different parts of the answer.		
B	Use paragraphs to organise the answer.		
C	Provide lots of detail, as many concepts as possible.		
D	Make the answer shorter.		

Activity 1: Using the mark scheme

Look at the question below:

Outline how the government could reduce the level of unemployment in the economy. (2 marks)

Now look at the mark scheme below.

1 mark for the identification of one measure the government could use, and 1 mark for some kind of development or example using the unemployment context.

Mark the two student responses to the question above. There are 2 marks available for each question.

Remember

To answer an 'Outline' question, you can make one point and give some development using sentences. These may be linked.

Student A:

Taxes

Lower interest rates

Investment

Mark awarded	Reasons

Student B:

The government could reduce unemployment by lowering taxes. This would give people more money to spend and so businesses would have to take on more workers.

Mark awarded	Reasons

Activity 2: Understanding the question

For the following question, look at the different student responses in the table below.

> Outline **one** problem a business might face by growing too large.   *(2 marks)*

Decide whether the student responses in the table below provide statements that are developed. If they do, place a tick in the second column. If they do not, place a cross in the second column.

In both cases, use the third column to explain the reasons behind your decision.

Response		Developed?	Reasons
A	If a business gets too big its costs will rise. Also, growing in size will make the business difficult to manage.		
B	By growing in size the business will have more employees. This will mean that the business is more difficult to manage.		
C	By being too big a business will have high costs. However, it will also have economies of scale and so it will not all be bad news. This is an example of economies of scale.		

Activity 3: Improve an answer

Look at the question below:

> Outline **one** way in which a strengthening of the exchange rate of the pound could affect a UK exporter.
>
> *(2 marks)*

Think about how each of the student answers below might be improved. The tables suggest possible improvements. Indicate with a tick or a cross in the second column whether each suggestion will improve the answer. In the right hand column offer reasons to support your decision.

Student A:

A strengthening of the exchange rate means that the pound will buy more of a foreign currency. By strengthening in value the exporters will be at a disadvantage. This is because their products will cost more for foreign customers. But it will mean that imports are cheaper.

	Suggested improvement	Does this help?	Reasons
A	Don't provide definitions of terms.		
B	Link together different parts of the answer.		
C	Use paragraphs to organise the answer.		
D	Provide lots of detail, as many concepts as possible.		
E	Provide one point and develop it.		

Student B:

The business will suffer as foreign consumers will face higher prices. Demand will therefore fall.

	Suggested improvement	Does this help?	Reasons
A	Link together different parts of the answer.		
B	Use paragraphs to organise the answer.		
C	Provide lots of detail, as many concepts as possible.		
D	Provide one point and develop it.		

Introduction to 'Describe' questions

'Describe' questions will be found mostly in **Sections A and B** of the exam paper.

To answer a 'Describe' question you need to make a number of unrelated points using sentences. In a 3-mark question you should make 3 points, or 1 or 2 points with some development; in a 4-mark question, you should make 4 points or 2 points with some development of each. 'Describe' questions allow you to use a definition as one of your points.

Most, but not all, 'Describe' questions make reference to a particular business. These questions must be answered in the context of that business, i.e. your answer must be capable of being linked to the particular business in the evidence, not just **any** business.

> **Hint**
>
> To help put an answer into context, think about the kind of product the business produces and who the competition is in the market place.

A student aiming for the top grades should try to score full marks in all 'Describe' questions.

A typical question without context

Describe why branding might be important to a business. (3 marks)

A 3-mark answer

Branding gives a business a clearer identity and personality. A brand is important because it makes your product stand out. Branding allows a company to successfully increase its prices.

Why does this response gain 3 marks?

There are three sentences. Each sentence says something different about why branding is important to a business, although the second sentence might be regarded as a development of the first. One mark is awarded for each valid sentence.

A typical question with context

Describe why developing a well known brand is important to the success of a business such as Amazon. (3 marks)

A 3-mark answer

Branding gives Amazon a clear identity and personality. Branding allows Amazon to stand out because Internet retailing is very competitive. Branding means that more people are likely to visit the website and buy Amazon products, increasing profit.

There are three sentences. Each sentence says something different about why branding is important to a business. The answer is also applied to the context of Amazon/Internet retailing. **Without this use of context the answer would have been worth only 2 marks.**

Activity 1: Using the mark scheme

Look at the question below:

Describe why it is important for Subway to differentiate its products. (3 marks)

Now look at the mark scheme for this question:

For 3 marks, development will clearly show the importance of product differentiation to Subway. Within the answer there will be three points made or two points with one being developed, with the answer rooted in the Subway/sandwich/fast food context. 2 marks are awarded for the points/development and 1 mark is awarded for the use of context.

Possible answers include:

- Increases sales/market share.
- Stands out against rivals, e.g. McDonald's.
- Enables the firm to add value.
- Allows the firm to charge higher prices without the loss of demand.
- Makes it harder for a new firm to set up in competition.
- Helps build a strong brand presence.

Use the mark scheme to mark the answer below. Place your score in the box below the answer.

Student A:

Differentiation allows a firm's products to stand out in the market place which means that the product is seen as being different or better than the competition. It can also give a firm a unique selling point.

Mark awarded = _____ /3

Do you think this answer can be improved? If you think it can, explain why in the space below:

....

....

....

....

....

Activity 2: Improve an answer

In the previous activity we looked at the following question:

> *Describe why it is important for Subway to differentiate its products.*   *(3 marks)*

Student A:

Differentiation allows a firm's products to stand out in the market place which means that the product is seen as being different or better than the competition. It can also give a firm a unique selling point.

Examiner's comments:

The answer scored 2 marks, since a point was made with some development and this was followed by another unrelated but relevant point. However the answer made no reference to Subway at all and, because Subway was mentioned in the question, the answer needs to be applied to the business stated.

In the student's answer some words have been highlighted in yellow. It is possible to replace these highlighted words with new words that will improve the answer, allowing it to be applied to what Subway does.

Fill in the gaps in the answer below with words that will allow the answer to become more closely associated with Subway. The first two gaps have been completed for you in red.

> *Differentiation allows* <u>Subway's baguettes</u> *to stand out in the* ....
>
> *which means that its* .... *are seen as being different or better than*
>
> *the competition like* .... *. Providing* ....
>
> *can also give Subway a unique selling point.*

Hint

In questions that include the name of a business, you must apply your answer to the business in question. This is one of the main reasons why many students do not gain full marks in 'Describe' questions.

Activity 3: Write an answer

Look at the questions below:

Question 1:

Describe a benefit to a business of improved worker motivation.   *(3 marks)*

Question 2:

Describe why a strong brand might be important to Apple.   *(3 marks)*

There is an **important difference** between these two questions and how they will be marked. Explain this difference in the space below:

....

....

....

....

....

You need to remember the following things when writing an answer to a 'Describe' question:

○ You need to write two to three separate points in sentences that do not need to be linked, although one point may be developed.

○ You can use a definition as one of the points.

○ In questions that refer to the name of a business, you have to apply your answer to that business.

 On a separate piece of paper, write an answer to both of the questions above. Give yourself no longer than 3 minutes to answer each question.

You or a friend can now mark the answers using the mark scheme on page 92.

Activity 1: Using the mark scheme

Look at the question below:

Describe the possible disadvantages for a business when it grows in size.   *(3 marks)*

Now look at the mark scheme for this question:

For 3 marks, development will clearly show understanding of the disadvantages of business growth. Within the answer there will be three points made or two points with one being developed.

Possible answers include:

- Potential problems if the business grows too quickly or becomes too 'big'.
- Possible diseconomies of scale as average costs of production rise.
- Increases in costs coincide with a less than proportionate increase in output.
- Businesses may be forced to increase prices.
- More difficult to manage.
- Communications more difficult.

Use the mark scheme to mark the answer below. Place your score in the box below the answer.

Student A:

One disadvantage of a business growing in size is diseconomies of scale. As the business grows it will be too big to manage and its costs will rise.

Mark awarded = [/3   ]

Do you think this answer can be improved? If you think it can, explain why in the space below:

....

....

....

....

....

....

Look at the question below:

Describe how a strengthening of the pound against other currencies might affect a UK export business.

(4 marks)

Student A:

The exchange rate is how much one currency is worth in terms of another. If the exchange rate strengthens, £1 will buy more of a foreign currency. Exporters will suffer, however, as their product will now cost more for foreign customers. This will also help importers who will be able to buy foreign goods more cheaply.

Examiner's comments:

The answer scored 3 marks, since a definition was provided (1 mark) plus two valid points about how a UK exporter will be affected. However, the answer does not focus on an exporter. The last sentence states how an importer might be affected. This is not the question!

It is possible to rewrite the answer, focusing on what an exporter does instead.

Look at another response. This also can be improved. Fill in the gaps in the answer below with words that will allow the answer to become more closely associated with a UK exporter.

A strong pound is .... for an exporter. This is because their

goods will be .... for foreign customers. However,

if the exporter has to import components or raw materials, it will ....

from the strong pound. This is because imports will now be relatively ....

This will bring down costs.

Remember

In questions that include the name of a business, or a specific business context, you must apply your answer to this context. This is one of the main reasons why students do not gain full marks in 'Describe' questions.

Activity 3: Write an answer

Look at the questions below:

> **Question 1:**
>
> *Describe a benefit to a business of low interest rates.* (3 marks)
>
> **Question 2:**
>
> *Describe how a business like McDonald's might measure its success.* (3 marks)

There is an **important difference** between these two questions and how they will be marked. Explain this difference in the space below:

....

....

....

....

....

....

You need to remember the following things when writing an answer to a 'Describe' question:

- You need to write two to three separate points in sentences that do not need to be linked, although one point may be developed.

- You can use a definition as one of the points.

- In questions that refer to the name of a business, you need to apply your answer to that business.

 On a separate piece of paper, write an answer to both of the above questions. Give yourself no longer than 3 minutes to answer each question.

You or a friend can now mark the answers using the mark scheme on page 92 .

Introduction to 'Explain' questions

'Explain' questions will be found in **all** sections of the exam paper.

To answer an 'Explain' question you need to make a number of linked, related points using sentences. All 'Explain' questions are worth 3 marks. Offering a definition at the start of your answer does **not** allow you.

Most, but not all, 'Explain' questions make reference to a particular business. These questions must be answered in the context of that business.

A student aiming for the top grades should try for full marks in any 'Explain' questions.

> **Hint**
>
> To make sure you write related points in your answer, try to use connective words at the start of the second and third sentences such as 'because', 'this leads to…', and 'as a result…'.

A typical question without context

Explain why an increase in the rate of interest might lead to a reduction in inflation. (3 marks)

A 3-mark answer

Raising interest rates will make loans more expensive. As a result, people will take out fewer loans. This leads to consumer spending going down, forcing firms to lower prices.

Why does this response gain 3 marks?

There are three sentences. Each sentence is linked together and logically explains why a rise in the rate of interest will cause a reduction in inflation. The answer makes good use of connective words and phrases, which are highlighted in red in the answer.

A typical question with context

*Explain **one** benefit to Sony of improving its productivity. (3 marks)*

A 3-mark answer

Increasing productivity means Sony can make more PlayStation 3 consoles in an hour. This results in the average cost of making each console going down. As a result, Sony can lower prices to out-compete Xbox.

Why does this response gain 3 marks?

There are three sentences. Each sentence is linked, explaining why higher productivity benefits Sony. There is good use of the Sony/PlayStation® 3 context. **Without this use of context the answer would have been worth only 2 marks.**

Activity 1: Understanding the exam question

The command word 'explain' is different from the command word 'describe'.

In order to meet the command word 'explain', sentences need to be **linked together** to answer the question. **A definition will not be awarded any marks.** This is because an 'Explain' question requires you to also demonstrate higher order skills of application and analysis rather than simply giving knowledge.

Look at the question below:

> *Explain* **one** *way in which a Just In Time (JIT) method of stock control might benefit a business such as McDonald's.* *(3 marks)*

In order to answer the question, you will need to do the following:

- Identify **one** way.

- Use two sentences to explain how the way will benefit McDonald's.

- Make sure you apply your answer to McDonald's or a similar fast-food restaurant.

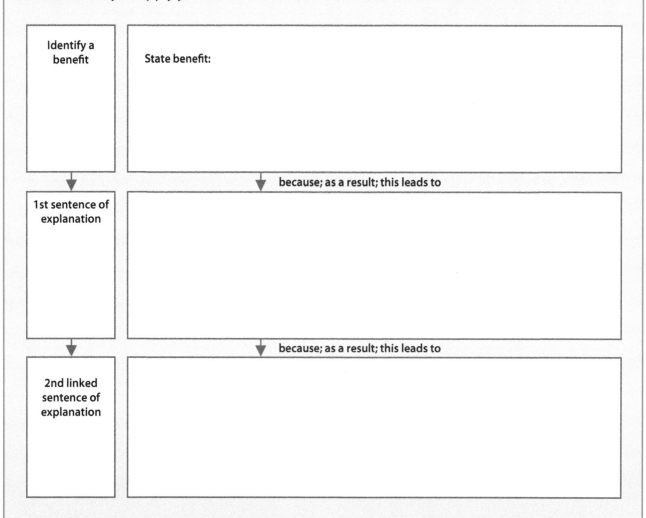

Use the grid below to create an answer:

Have you used words like 'burgers', 'fast food' or 'McDonald's' in your answer? If not you might not gain all 3 marks because you have not applied your answer to the business in the question.

Activity 2: Using the mark scheme

Look at the question below:

Explain why strong cash flow is important to a supermarket such as Lidl.   *(3 marks)*

Now look at the mark scheme for this question:

For 3 marks, development will clearly show the importance of strong cash flow. Within the answer there will be at least two clearly identifiable strands of explanation with the answer applied to a Lidl/supermarket context. Two marks are awarded for the links and 1 mark is awarded for the use of context.

Possible answers include:

- Prevents failure (especially in recession).
- Prevents the need for loans/overdrafts.
- Can pay bills when they fall due.
- Improves financial management.
- Improves liquidity/working capital (although this is not on the specification, it could be an answer some candidates give and would be credited).

Use the mark scheme to mark the answer below. Place your score in the box below the answer.

Student A:

Cash flow is the record of cash inflows and cash outflows over time. Having strong cash flow will make it less likely that Lidl will run out of cash. As a result, Lidl will be able to pay its suppliers on time.

Mark awarded = [/3]

In the space below, justify your mark and suggest how the answer can be improved.

Justify your mark:

....

....

....

....

Improvements:

....

....

....

....

Activity 3: Improve an answer

Look at the question below:

*Explain **one** benefit to Co-operative Food of being an ethical business.* (3 marks)

Student A:

Being ethical means that Co-operative Food considers all of the stakeholders that are affected by the company's activities. It has a moral obligation to do the right thing. Being ethical is important because it means that the world is not polluted and people are not exploited. Being ethical will improve Co-operative Food's branding a lot.

This answer could have been improved if the student had:

- started by highlighting **one** benefit to Co-operative Food of being ethical

- written two linked sentences of explanation

- made sure they applied their answer to Co-operative Food/supermarkets.

> **Remember**
> To make sure your answer is applied to Co-operative Food, think about what Co-operative Food sells and who its competition is.

Using the final sentence of the student's answer as your starting point, improve this answer so that it gets better marks, by explaining why being ethical will benefit Co-operative Food.

Being ethical will improve Co-operative Food's branding a lot. This results in ....

....

....

....

....

As a result, Co-operative Food can ....

....

....

....

....

....

The command word 'explain' is different from the command word 'describe'.

In order to meet the command word 'explain', sentences need to be **linked together** to answer the question. **A definition will not be awarded any marks.** This is because an 'Explain' question requires you to also demonstrate higher order skills of application and analysis rather than simply giving knowledge.

Look at the question below:

> *Explain **one** way in which a business might benefit from economies of scale.*   *(3 marks)*

In order to answer the question, you will need to do the following:

○ Identify **one** way.

○ Use two sentences to explain how this way will benefit a business.

Use the grid below to create an answer:

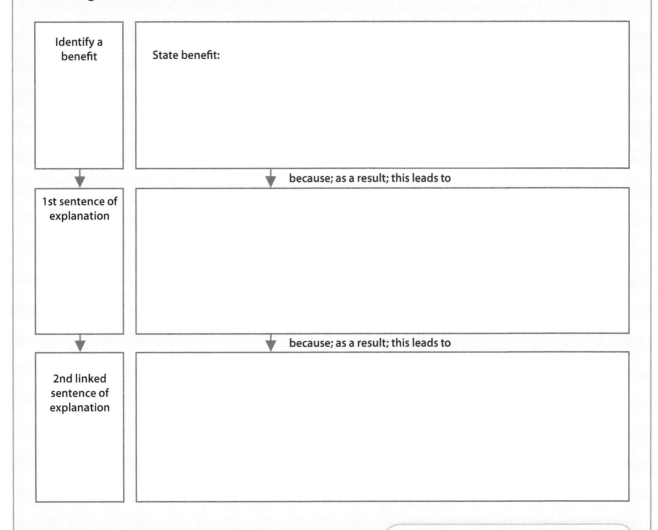

Identify a benefit	State benefit:

because; as a result; this leads to

1st sentence of explanation	

because; as a result; this leads to

2nd linked sentence of explanation	

Hint

Don't be too general in your answer. For example, stating that 'this will lead to higher profits' is not enough. You need to **explain** the impact.

Activity 2: Using the mark scheme

Look at the question below:

The Single European Market (SEM) in the European Union (EU) has led to the development of free trade between its members. It has led to an improvement in living standards amongst member countries. The EU places trade restrictions on non-member countries.

*Explain **one** reason why the EU might want to restrict trade.*　　　　(3 marks)

Now look at the mark scheme for this question:

For 3 marks, development will clearly show the importance of trade restrictions. Within the answer there will be at least two clearly identifiable strands of explanation with the answer rooted in an EU context. 1 mark is awarded for the reason and 2 marks for the explanation, which is based on the context of the question.

Possible reasons include:

- To encourage the free movement of goods and services only between members.
- To stop the inflow of goods and services which might threaten infant industries.
- Free trade threatens the standard of living of member populations.
- To maintain employment.

Use the mark scheme to mark the answer below. Place your score in the box below the answer.

Student A:
The EU is a region which allows free trade between member states to take place. The EU restricts trade so employment in member countries is high and therefore standard of living is high.

Mark awarded = 　　| 　　/3　　|

In the space below, justify your mark and suggest how the answer can be improved.

Justify your mark:

....

....

....

Improvements:

....

....

....

Activity 3: Improve an answer

Look at the question below:

> *Explain **one** effect of inflation on a business* (3 marks)

Student A:

Inflation is the general rise in prices in an economy. The UK has an inflation target of 2%. If it increases above this level then the Bank of England will increase interest rates. One effect of high interest rates is that loans become more expensive for businesses. One impact of high inflation on a business is that its running costs are likely to increase.

This answer could have been improved if the student had:

- started by highlighting **one** effect of inflation on a business

- written two linked sentences of explanation

- made sure they focused their answer on the effects on a business.

Using the final sentence of the student's answer as your starting point, improve this answer so that it gets better marks, by explaining how inflation will affect a business.

> **Remember**
> Stay focused! Think about the effects of inflation – rising prices – **on the business**.

One impact of high inflation on a business is that its running costs are likely to increase.

This may mean that ....

....

....

....

....

Because of ....

....

....

....

....

....

....

Introduction to choice questions

Section A or Section B will often include at least one choice question which is worth 6 (and sometimes 8) marks. The first part of the question provides the business or economic context. The second part asks you to decide which is the best method or factor from the context. There is no right or wrong answer in terms of the choice you make. So long as you can **justify** your choice.

How will I be marked?

This question is worth 6 marks. A student aiming for the top grades should try to score full marks on this type of question. To get good marks you need to:

- make a decision about which is the 'best' method or decision

- give two developed explanations containing linked statements that help to justify your decision

- use appropriate business concepts and terms

- provide a conclusion.

> **Hint**
> Using 2–3 paragraphs will help you to structure the type of response needed.

Note: You can refer to both methods in your answer – but you do not need to do this to answer the question correctly.

A typical question

Improving the quality of a product and improving productivity are two ways in which a business like McDonald's might become more competitive.

Which of these two methods do you think would be most effective in improving the competitiveness of a business such as McDonald's and why? (6 marks)

A 6-mark answer

McDonald's should choose to improve productivity in their restaurants. They could do this by training its workers to do jobs more quickly, which will mean customers will receive better and quicker service. As people today are often very busy this will mean they will choose McDonald's over other takeaways.

Furthermore, by improving productivity of workers, McDonald's will be able to reduce average costs. This means that prices might be able to be reduced, and therefore they become even more competitive.

In conclusion, increasing productivity is the most effective way of increasing competitiveness, since increasing quality is pointless as people do not associate McDonald's with high quality burgers.

Why does this response gain 6 marks?

This response gets 6 marks because the student gives a judgement and then offers a method of improving productivity and a consequence of this. This is then justified by giving a reason.

A second reason is then given with a consequence and a judgement ('even more competitive…'). The explanations are made up of linked statements, and make use of linking phrases like 'this will mean…'

Also, business terms – training and average costs – are used in the answer. The student then provides a summary conclusion which is based on the analysis.

Note: If you have an 8-mark choice question, exactly the same principles apply as detailed above but you may need to provide more than two reasons/causes/consequences along with a more developed conclusion in context.

Remember

There is no right or wrong answer. You can gain 6 marks by arguing for either of the two methods. If you had approached this by explaining why improving quality would be a better strategy than higher productivity then this could also gain 6 marks. An example of this approach follows on page 49.

Activity 1: Understanding the exam question

In the introduction to choice questions, we looked at the following question:

Improving the quality of a product and improving productivity are two ways in which a business like McDonald's might become more competitive.

Which of these two methods do you think would be most effective in improving the competitiveness of a business such as McDonald's and why? (6 marks)

In the table below there are four statements about McDonald's. On a scale of 1–5, with 5 being very important and 1 being not important at all, rate how important each factor is likely to be to McDonald's customers. Tick a box to highlight your rating for each factor.

Factor		1	2	3	4	5
A	Low waiting time					
B	Best cuts of meat					
C	Low prices					
D	Attractive packaging of food					

By thinking about what is important to McDonald's customers you are better able to make a choice as to whether quality or increased productivity is the most important factor in improving McDonald's competitiveness.

Now decide whether each statement is related to productivity or product quality by ticking the appropriate box in the table below:

Statement		Productivity	Quality of product
A	Low waiting time		
B	Best cuts of meat		
C	Lowest prices		
D	Attractive packaging		

By thinking like this you are more likely to be able to write an answer which is in **context** and be able to justify your choice with a high quality explanation.

Activity 2: Using the mark scheme

Look at the student response for the question repeated below.

Improving the quality of a product and improving productivity are two ways in which a business like McDonald's might become more competitive.

Which of these two methods do you think would be most effective in improving the competitiveness of a business such as McDonald's and why? (6 marks)

Try to work out how many marks the answer below was awarded using the mark scheme provided. The answer has reached Level 3, but should it be awarded 5 or 6 marks? Briefly give reasons for your decision in the table provided below.

Level	Descriptor
Level 3 5–6 marks	A judgement/point is given on one or both issues (productivity and quality) with some development/support, which includes at least **two** reasons/causes/consequences etc. which are in context. At the top of this level there will be a conclusion drawn from the analysis and the answer will be in a McDonald's context.

Student A:

By improving the quality of its product McDonald's can stand out compared to other firms. This will allow it to sell more of its products and gain a strong brand image. If its image is strong it can charge more for its goods and services and make larger profits, making the firm more competitive.

Productivity is how many goods and services a firm can make in a period of time. If McDonald's makes more of its product in an hour, the wages paid to its staff will be divided up over more units of output. As a result the average cost of each item will be reduced, giving McDonald's a greater profit margin on each item sold.

As a result, improving productivity is most important because it allows profits to be increased much more quickly.

Mark awarded	Reasons

Activity 3: Improve an answer

In order to improve the sample answer in Activity 2, use the table below to consider its strengths/weaknesses.

Element of answer		Strong	Weak	Explanation
A	Use of the McDonald's context.			
B	Paragraph structure.			
C	Use of terminology.			
D	Number of reasons/causes/ consequences.			

Read the following sample answer:

Student B:

By improving the quality of its product McDonald's can stand out compared to rival fast food companies such as Burger King and KFC. This will allow it to sell more burgers and gain a strong brand image. If its image is strong it can charge more for its burgers and make larger profits, making McDonald's more competitive.

Productivity is how many burgers McDonald's can make in a period of time. If McDonald's makes more burgers in an hour, the wages paid to its staff will be divided up over more units of output. As a result the average cost of each burger will be reduced, giving McDonald's a greater profit margin on each burger sold.

As a result, improving productivity is the most important factor in improving McDonald's competitiveness because McDonald's focus on fast food which is aimed at consumers who want to buy food in a hurry. Since the prices paid are quite low consumers are not really looking for high quality food and really want their food much more quickly. Improving productivity allows this to happen.

Using a highlighter pen, highlight every word or phrase that puts the answer into a fast food/McDonald's context. Do the same for the answer you marked in Activity 2.

Notice the difference between the amount you have highlighted on the first response in Activity 2 and the amount highlighted on this response. Both are good answers, but the second response has demonstrated more use of context, which is why it gains all 6 marks.

Activity 4: Build an answer

Read the question below and look at the mark scheme.

Transporting goods and services long distances creates pollution and environmental damage. Tesco faced lots of criticism from newspapers following its decision to stock fruit which has been grown in Africa, rather than the UK.

Following this criticism, Tesco could respond in one of the following ways:

Option 1: *Do nothing*

Option 2: *Only sell fruit grown in the UK*

In your opinion which option should Tesco adopt and why? (6 marks)

Level	Descriptor
Level 3 5–6 marks	A judgement/point is given on one or both issues (Option 1 and Option 2) with some development/support, which includes at least **two** reasons/causes/consequences etc. which are in context. At the top of this level there will be a conclusion drawn from the analysis and the answer will be in a fruit/Tesco context.

In order to build an answer you need to get the structure right. This will help you to do the things required for your answer to reach Level 3.

 This can be done using three paragraphs. Use the guide below and fill in each step, following the instructions from the mark scheme to build your answer on a separate sheet.

Paragraph 1:

Write a paragraph on the 'selling only fruit grown in the UK' option that includes at least **two** reasons why. Try to use business terminology to express yourself.

Paragraph 2:

Write a paragraph on the 'do nothing' option that includes at least **two** reasons why. Try to use business terminology to express yourself.

Paragraph 3:

Make a decision as to which option is best. Remember to explain your reasons and make sure you use the fruit/Tesco context in your conclusion.

Activity 1: Understanding the exam question

Read the following question:

Two ways in which lorry companies can be helped when the economy is in recession are to:

- *reduce the tax on fuel*

- *reduce interest rates.*

In your opinion, which of these two ways will be most effective in helping a lorry company during a recession? Justify your answer. (6 marks)

For each of the following three student responses, indicate with a tick or a cross whether they include 'linked' explanations.

Response		Linked?	Reasons
A	Interest rates are the amount charged by banks when individuals or businesses borrow money. Lower interest rates will help lorry businesses to reduce fixed costs.		
B	Lower interest rates will help lorry companies, especially if the business has loans on which it pays interest. This will help to reduce fixed costs, but only of those businesses which have loans. Lower fixed costs can mean higher profits.		
C	Lower taxes on fuel will certainly help lorry companies by reducing their variable costs. Lower taxes will also affect customers, who may have more money to spend on things.		

Activity 2: Using the mark scheme

Look at the student response below for the question shown on the previous page. Decide how many marks you would give this answer. Briefly give reasons for your decision in the box provided. Use the mark scheme provided below to help you.

Level	Descriptor
Level 3 5–6 marks	A judgement/point is given on one or both issues (lower fuel taxes) with some development/support, which includes at least **two** reasons/causes/consequences etc. which are in context. At the top of this level there will be a conclusion drawn from the analysis and the answer will be in a lower interest rates context.

Student A:

The thing that will be most effective in helping a lorry company during recession will be to reduce the tax on fuel. As fuel is the main variable cost used by a transport business, a cut in tax will mean lower costs. This will mean that the business will make more profit.

Lower interest rates will also help, especially if the business has loans on which it pays interest. This will help to reduce fixed costs, but only of those businesses which have loans.

Remember

To answer the question you need to:

- make a decision about which you think is the 'best' method or decision
- give two developed explanations containing linked statements which help to justify your decision
- use appropriate business concepts and terms
- provide a conclusion.

Note: You may refer to both methods in your answer – but you do not need to do this to correctly answer the question.

Hint

Read the question closely. How well does this response answer the question?

Mark awarded	Reasons

Activity 3: Improve an answer

One way to improve your exam technique is to look at responses to exam questions and suggest how they might be improved. Look at the student response below and come up with possible improvements, using the general mark scheme on the previous page.

The response is based on the following question:

Pollution and the use of non-renewable resources are two drawbacks of economic growth. Which of these do you think is most serious and why? (6 marks)

Student A:

Economic growth is measured by GDP and is an indicator of the standard of living in a country. The higher the level of GDP, the better the standard of living in that particular country. However, economic growth is not always a good thing. Two reasons are pollution and the use of non-renewable resources. Pollution is caused by businesses and can cause negative externalities. When GDP rises, more factories are producing more output and this causes their levels of pollution to rise. Therefore, pollution and economic growth are definitely linked. Non-renewable resources are those such as oil and copper which are limited in supply and will eventually run out. When economic growth takes place, countries use more natural resources, for example in manufacturing industries. Therefore, economic growth causes the use of such resources. However, when resources are used more, the price will increase and this will cause businesses and consumers to search for alternatives. It is therefore unlikely that resources will be completely used up. Pollution, though, will always occur when businesses produce more, and this is therefore the most serious effect of economic growth.

The table below suggests possible improvements. Indicate with a tick or a cross in the second column whether each one will help take this response to the next level. In the right hand column offer reasons to support your decision.

	Suggested improvement	Does this help?	Reasons
A	Use paragraphs to organise the response.		
B	Make a decision in the first paragraph then justify it.		
C	Begin with definitions of key terms.		
D	Provide lots of detail, bringing in many different concepts.		
E	Don't make a specific judgement. Instead, say it could be either.		

Activity 4: Build an answer

Look at the question below:

Two disadvantages to a country like Kenya from being outside the EU include:

- *a loss of revenue for businesses*
- *a fall in living standards.*

Which of these do you think is the most damaging to Kenya's economy and why?

(6 marks)

 The following flow chart shows you the steps you should take in preparing an answer to this question. You will then build your own answer to this question by following these steps on a separate sheet.

Step 1

Identify which factor will be most damaging to Kenya.

Remember
There is no right or wrong answer.

Step 2

Get straight into the question. State your decision and give at least one reason/cause /consequence. Provide linked statements. Make sure you use business/economics terminology as part of your paragraph.

Step 3

Write a paragraph on the second factor, and give at least one reason/cause/ consequence why this might be damaging to the Kenyan economy. Make sure you use business/economics terminology in this paragraph.

Step 4

Provide a final, short paragraph arriving at a conclusion, making sure you focus your answer around Kenya. Say why your identified factor is more important than the other. Don't simply repeat what you have already said. This is your chance to demonstrate original thinking.

Remember
This is just one strategy for tackling this type of question. You need not make reference to both factors.

Complete the following grid to plan your answer to this question. You could use bullet points to summarise how you would explain each cause.

A	Make a judgement	The most damaging effect will be…
B	Analyse and evaluate	The reason for this is… This is very important because…
C	Analyse how the other effect will impact on Kenya	…will also…
D	Analyse and evaluate	The reason for this is… This is very important because…
E	Conclusion	

Introduction to 'Discuss' questions

'Discuss' questions will be found in **Section C** of the exam paper, but could also be in Section B.

> **Note:** This type of 'Discuss' question may not appear on every question paper. This is provided as guidance for when such a question does appear!

All 'Discuss' questions will be linked to a case study at the start of Section C, so you will need to write in context throughout your answer. Most 'Discuss' questions refer to a particular problem/benefit/opportunity faced by a business or an economy. To answer the question you have to judge how important that problem/benefit/opportunity is compared with at least one other problem/benefit/opportunity. 'Discuss' questions are worth either 6 or 8 marks.

To answer a 'Discuss' question you need to write up to **three** paragraphs. The first paragraph should explain why the problem/benefit/opportunity highlighted in the question is important. The second paragraph should explain why a different problem/benefit/opportunity might be more or less important. The final paragraph should contain a judgement as to which of the two problems/benefits/opportunities is the most important and why.

> **Hint**
>
> Make sure you write a conclusion and that you write an answer using the context provided in the case study.

A student aiming for the top grades should try to score at least 5/6 or 7/8 marks on this type of question.

A typical question

Discuss the importance of developing new products in allowing a business like Pepsi to increase its competitiveness. (6 marks)

A 6-mark answer

New products will allow Pepsi to demonstrate innovation in the soft drinks market. This might encourage consumers to try its new drinks. This will increase Pepsi's market share and give it a competitive advantage over Coca-Cola.

However, innovation is just one way Pepsi could become more competitive. A better way would be to increase the branding of Pepsi so that it is more widely known compared to Coca-Cola. This is because it is difficult to successfully develop new cola drinks since any innovation is going to change the taste of the drink and this might put consumers off.

In the short-term, focusing on branding and keeping the price of Pepsi low might be more successful in allowing Pepsi to gain competitiveness, especially when it faces such strong competition from Coca-Cola. In the longer-term, new cola drinks may be more important in increasing Pepsi's competitiveness, especially ones that are healthier. Pepsi need to be careful in making new drinks which taste as good as their regular version though.

Why does this response gain 6 marks?

'Discuss' questions are marked using a 'levels of response' mark scheme. The top of the mark scheme (5–6 marks) can be seen below:

Level	Descriptor
Level 3 5–6 marks	Reference to two reasons is given with development of each. A judgement/point is given with some development which includes at least two causes/consequences, etc. for each reason and may include some comparison between the two. Candidates at this level will weigh up the importance of new product development against another factor which may be more/less important. Answers at the top of this level will refer to the Pepsi context.

The answer above scored 6 marks (top level 3) because there was a paragraph explaining why new cola products could be important in giving Pepsi a competitive advantage. This was then contrasted with a different factor that could increase Pepsi's competitiveness. In the final paragraph a judgement was made and supported. The answer had a clear Pepsi/soft drink focus, allowing it to reach the top level of the mark scheme.

Activity 1: Understanding the exam question

In 'Discuss' questions you need to be **evaluative** and **analytical**. This involves making a judgement between **two** problems/opportunities/benefits faced by a company and offering some support in the form of reasons, causes, consequences, etc.

Look at the question below:

> Affinity is a small publishing company that produces guide books containing short walks for parents with small children and prams. Discuss the benefits to Affinity of improved motivation of its employees. *(6 marks)*

Use the table below to list four benefits of improved employee motivation. Once you have made your list, tick a box in the table next to each benefit to highlight how important that benefit is to Affinity (1 = not important, 5 = most important).

Benefit of improved employee motivation	1	2	3	4	5

Now choose the most important benefit and a benefit that you have ranked as less important, and fill in the table below explaining why you made that decision.

Most important benefit	Reason

Less important benefit	Reason

You now have the content for a high quality conclusion. The best way to write this is to state that one of the benefits is more important than the other, and then explain why. There is no right answer to this, but make sure you give reasons to support your judgement. Remember, this has to be applied to the business in the question.

Remember

It is always good technique to use a very important benefit and then a benefit which is not really important at all in your first two paragraphs. This makes it easier for you to make the comparison and draw an appropriate conclusion in the third paragraph. Also, don't forget to offer evaluation throughout, where possible.

Activity 2: Using the mark scheme

Look at the question below:

Discuss the importance of promotion as a method of increasing the motivation of workers at KFC.　　　　　　　　　　　　　　　　　　　　　*(6 marks)*

Now look at the mark scheme for this question:

Level	Descriptor
Level 3 5–6 marks	Reference as to why promotion is important is given with development. A judgement/point is given with some development which includes at least **two** causes/consequences, etc. and may include some reference to another factor as a means of comparison. Answers at the top of this level will refer to the context.

Use the mark scheme to mark the student answer below, placing your score in the box below the answer:

Student A:

Promotion is a very important way of increasing motivation at KFC. The job at KFC is a hard one, especially during busy periods around lunch time. Workers who do well and can cope with the stress of a busy fast food restaurant will want to be recognised by the company they work for and the chance of being promoted to restaurant manager will be very attractive to them and boost their motivation.

However, for some workers, promotion will not be important. This is because KFC employs lots of students, and these students have no interest in staying with KFC after they leave school or university. As a result, a higher wage is much more likely to motivate these workers than the chance of promotion would.

The extent to which promotion motivates a worker at KFC depends on the type of person and where they are in Maslow's hierarchy. An A-level student is probably only working to gain extra money and therefore will not be motivated at all by the chance of promotion. On the other hand a person who has been with KFC for four or five years and has already been promoted will probably find the chance of further promotion much more attractive and will work harder to achieve it.

Mark awarded = | /6

Justify your mark in the space below and suggest any possible improvements.

....

....

....

....

....

Activity 3: Build an answer

Look at the question below:

Discuss the benefits to BMW of improving its productivity. (6 marks)

Now look at the mark scheme for this question:

Level	Descriptor
Level 3 5–6 marks	Reference to **more than one** benefit is given with development of each. A judgement/point is given with some development which includes at least **two** reasons/causes/consequences, etc. for each benefit and may include a comparison between the two. Answers at the top of this level will refer to the BMW/car context.

An obvious structure is to use three paragraphs. The first **two** paragraphs develop benefits of BMW improving its productivity, offering **two** reasons/causes/consequences of doing so for each benefit. Use the spaces below to help structure the first two paragraphs of an answer.

Paragraph 1:   Benefit 1:...

Reasons/causes/consequences 1:...

....

Reasons/causes/consequences 2:...

....

Paragraph 2:   Benefit 2:...

Reasons/causes/consequences 1:...

....

Reasons/causes/consequencse 2:...

....

Once you have completed the structure for the first two paragraphs, you need to consider what you are going to put in the final paragraph. Use the table below to consider which of the two benefits is the most important, explaining why.

Most important benefit	Reason

Comparing the two benefits and stating that one is more important than the other, and then explaining why, is a good way to demonstrate the analysis and evaluation that will allow you to reach Level 3 in the mark scheme.

Remember

Have you mentioned cars, BMW or one of BMW's competitors in what you have written? If you have not convincingly applied your answer to BMW, you will get fewer marks.

Read the evidence and then look at the question below:

> Poundland is a chain of discount stores that was set up in 1990. Everything sold in its stores is priced at £1. They sell everything from binoculars to bread, but the selling price is always the same. During the recession, the number of people shopping in Poundland increased. Retail experts believe this is because people were attracted by its simple pricing strategy of selling everything for £1.
>
> *Discuss the importance of advertising in allowing Poundland to improve its profits.* *(6 marks)*

You need to remember the following things when writing an answer to this 'Discuss' question:

○ You need to write **three** paragraphs.

○ The first paragraph should explain why advertising is important in allowing Poundland to improve its profits.

○ The second paragraph should explain why a different factor may be important in allowing Poundland to improve its profits.

○ In the final paragraph you need to make a judgement as to whether advertising or your second factor is of greater importance in allowing Poundland to improve its profits, explaining why.

○ Your answer must be applied to the context, i.e. Poundland.

 On a separate piece of paper, write an answer to this question. Give yourself no longer than 6 minutes to do this. It would be a good idea to divide this time up into 2 minutes for each of the three paragraphs.

You or a friend can now mark the answer using the mark scheme on page 92.

In 'Discuss' questions you need to be **evaluative** and **analytical**. This involves making a judgement about problems/opportunities/benefits faced by a company and offering some support in the form of reasons, causes, consequences, etc.

Look at the question below:

> *When a business has a market share of 25% it can be classed as a monopoly. Microsoft has a monopoly position in the market for computer operating systems.*
>
> *Discuss the view that monopoly is always bad for consumers.* (6 marks)

As a first step to tackling this question, identify two advantages and two disadvantages that monopoly may have to consumers. Use the table below to list the advantages and disadvantages of monopoly. One disadvantage has been done for you.

Once you have made your list, tick a box in the table next to each benefit to highlight how important this effect is for consumers (1 = not important, 5 = most important).

> **Hint**
>
> This will help you to decide what your answer will be.

Disadvantages	1	2	3	4	5
1. Can charge high prices as there is no competition.					
2.					

Advantages	1	2	3	4	5
1.					
2.					

Now choose the most important effect and one which you have ranked as less important, and fill in the table below explaining why you made that decision.

Most important effect	Reason

Less important effect	Reason

You now have the content for a high quality conclusion. The best way to write this is to state that one of the effects is more important than the other, and then explain why. There is no right answer to this but make sure you give reasons to support your judgement. This has to be worded around the context in the question.

> **Remember**
>
> It is always good technique to use a very important effect and then an effect which is not really important at all in your first two paragraphs. This makes it easier for you to make the comparison and draw an appropriate conclusion in the third paragraph. Also, don't forget to offer evaluation throughout, where possible.

Activity 2: Using the mark scheme

Look at the question below:

> *Businesses use the marketing mix – product, price, promotion and place – to help achieve their aims. Discuss the importance of promotion as a method of increasing the sales at KFC.*
>
> *(6 marks)*

Now look at the mark scheme for this question:

Level	Descriptor
Level 3 5–6 marks	Reference as to why promotion is important is given some development which includes at least **two** reasons/causes/consequences, etc. and may include some reference to another factor as a means of comparison (balance). Answers at the top of this level will refer to the context.

Use the mark scheme to mark the student answer provided below, placing your score in the box below the answer:

Student A:

Promotion is a very important way of increasing sales at KFC. The market is very competitive and so KFC needs to make sure its customers are aware. It will also have to offer promotions and offers to ensure it competes with McDonald's 'Happy Meals', for example.

However, there are other factors which will help KFC to increase sales. It may have an excellent promotion campaign, but if its prices are too high then it will not get any sales. Also, if the product is poor quality it is likely to suffer due to high quality competitors.

The extent to which promotion is the most important 'P' depends on the business. It is certainly important when lots of competition exists. In a monopoly there is less need for promotion.

Mark awarded = [/6]

Justify your mark in the space below and suggest any possible improvements.

....

....

....

....

....

....

....

Activity 3: Build an answer

Look at the question below:

Discuss the benefits to BMW of increasing in size. *(6 marks)*

Now look at the mark scheme for this question:

Level	Descriptor
Level 3 5–6 marks	Reference to **more than one** benefit is given with development of each. A judgement/point is given with some development which includes at least **two** reasons/causes/consequences, etc. for each benefit and may include a comparison between benefits. Answers at the top of this level will refer to the BMW/car context.

An obvious structure is to use three paragraphs. The first **two** paragraphs develop benefits of BMW increasing in size with up **two** reasons/causes/consequences of doing so for each. Use the spaces below to help structure the first two paragraphs of an answer.

Paragraph 1: Benefit 1:..

Reasons/causes/consequences 1:...

....

Reasons/causes/consequences 2:...

....

Paragraph 2: Benefit 2:..

Reasons/causes/consequences 1:...

....

Reasons/causes/consequencse 2:...

Once you have completed the structure for the first two paragraphs, you now need to consider what you are going to put in the final paragraph. Use the table below to consider which benefit is the most important, explaining why.

Most important benefit	Reason

Comparing benefits and stating that one is more important than the other, and then explaining why, is a good way to demonstrate the analysis and evaluation that will allow you to reach Level 3 in the mark scheme.

Remember

Have you mentioned cars, BMW or one of BMW's competitors in what you have written? If you have not convincingly applied your answer to BMW, you will get fewer marks.

Read the evidence and then look at the question below:

NEW RULES TO REDUCE BINGE DRINKING

Pubs, bars and shops face new rules aimed at reducing binge drinking. The government is worried about the cost of alcohol-related illness and the negative externalities associated with binge drinking.

One of the reasons given for the rise in binge drinking is the low price of alcohol. Some supermarkets are charging as little as 22p a can for their own brand beer. Many pubs run special offers including 2 for 1, and happy hours. In addition, the fact that incomes are rising means more people can afford to buy alcohol.

Discuss the effectiveness of high taxes as the best way to reduce binge drinking.

(6 marks)

You need to remember the following things when writing an answer to this 'Discuss' question:

- You need to write **three** paragraphs.

- The first paragraph should explain how high taxes may be an effective method in addressing the problem of binge drinking.

- The second paragraph should explain why a different method may be successful in addressing the problem of binge drinking.

- In the final paragraph you need to make a judgement as to which method will be the most successful, explaining why.

- Your answer must be applied to the context in the question, i.e. binge drinking.

 On a separate piece of paper, write an answer to this question. Give yourself no longer than 6 minutes to do this. It would be a good idea to divide this time up into 2 minutes for each of the three paragraphs.

You or a friend can now mark the answer using the mark scheme on page 93.

Introduction to 'Assess' questions

'Assess' questions typically appear in **Sections B and C** of the exam paper.

'Assess' questions will be linked to a business or economic context. Most refer to a particular problem/benefit/opportunity faced by a business or an economy. To answer the question you have to offer a **balanced** answer and/or attach some value to the points you are making, which show your ability to 'weigh up' an issue and make a judgement about how important or significant it is. 'Assess' questions are worth between 8 and 10 marks.

Note: 8- or 10-mark questions which use the command word 'Evaluate' require the same approach as 'Assess' questions.

How will I be marked?

A student aiming for the top grades should try to score at least 7/8 or 8/10 marks on this type of question.

To answer the question, you need to:

○ explain at least two effects

○ use appropriate business and economic terms

○ organise your answer into paragraphs: the first paragraph should explain why the issue highlighted in the question is important; the second paragraph should explain why the issue might be more or less important or give an alternative viewpoint

○ include a judgement in the final paragraph as to which of the two effects is the most important and why. Consider whether the 'it depends' rule can be used

○ ensure the judgement contains at least two reasons/causes and consequences.

You will not gain any marks for providing definitions of terms.

Hint

In your answer, think about using the phrase 'it depends'. Explain briefly that the decisions you arrive at in your response often depend on certain factors or assumptions.

Using 'it depends' in your conclusion will help you avoid providing responses which tend to repeat what you have already said.

A typical question

Princess Yachts International plc sells 15% of its yachts to the USA.

Assess the effects a strong pound might have on Princess Yachts plc's profits. (8 marks)

An 8-mark answer

A strong pound will reduce the cost of importing materials for Princess Yachts. This will help reduce its variable costs and so improve its profits. The size of the benefit will depend on how much Princess Yachts imports and how far the pound strengthens.

> 'It depends' rule used.

However, as Princess Yachts exports its finished products, the strong pound will be a problem. It will mean that the price of its boats will be higher for foreign consumers. This may lead to lower sales revenue which could cause a fall in profits. However, as people who buy such boats are usually very rich, they may not be bothered about a rise in the price. They are less price sensitive than normal consumers.

> Clear structure of paragraphs. Student offers balance here.

In conclusion, the overall effect on Princess Yachts' profits depends on the balance between the lower cost of imports and the negative effect on exports. Given the nature of the product (i.e. bought by the rich) it is likely that the lower costs it will gain from the strong pound may well mean it benefits overall.

> Concluding third paragraph.

> 'It depends' rule used.

Why does this response gain 8 marks?

This response gets 8 marks because the student offers a balanced answer which explains both how this business might benefit from a strong pound, and how it may suffer. It offers development of at least two effects of a strong pound on Princess Yachts.

The student uses plenty of business terms. It is well structured using paragraphs. It is clear that the second paragraph provides balance as it begins with the word 'However'.

The student also shows good understanding of the topic. For example, the student states: 'A strong pound will reduce the cost of importing materials to make its boats from abroad. This will help reduce its variable costs and so improve its profits.' The student clearly understands that a strong pound will benefit an importer, and then shows a clear grasp of how this might impact on profit. This is required by the question. The candidate also shows their ability to evaluate by attaching a value to the effects using the 'it depends' rule.

A clear, original conclusion is provided which does not simply repeat what has already been said but makes a clear judgement.

Activity 1: Understanding the exam question

'Assess' questions require you to show **balance** and/or place a value on points you make. For each of the questions below you are provided with an argument. Provide an opposing (balancing) argument for each one and place a value on the argument.

Question 1:

Sony is a large Japanese electronic company. It manufactures televisions, DVD players and music players. Due to competition Sony has had to close several factories, making workers unemployed.

Assess the impact of job losses on the motivation of the remaining Sony employees.

(8 marks)

Remember

A good way of showing balance is to begin a paragraph with 'however'.

Argument	Balancing argument
With so many Sony workers losing their jobs, the workers that remain in the business will be scared of losing their jobs as well. This will mean that the remaining workers will be demotivated because they are no longer having their security needs met.	*However,* .... *But this depends on* ....

Question 2:

First Great Western is a train operating company that runs trains in the south-west of England and Wales. Its drivers are rewarded with a good salary and a range of fringe benefits, including a number of free rail tickets for their families and a free uniform.

Assess the likely importance of fringe benefits in allowing First Great Western to recruit more staff.

(8 marks)

Argument	Balancing argument
Fringe benefits will make a worker feel more valued by a business and will attract people to work for First Great Western. This is because the free uniform and rail tickets mean that the worker and his/her family will not have to spend their own money on these items. Therefore it is similar to boosting the worker's pay.	*However,* .... *But this depends on* ....

Activity 2: How do I use the 'it depends' rule?

In the previous activity we looked at how to bring balance into an answer. In this activity we are going to look at another important aspect of meeting the command word 'assess' or 'evaluate' and that is the use of the 'it depends' rule.

To answer the question, you will need to arrive at a clear conclusion. However, it is not enough simply to repeat what you have already said. For example: 'In conclusion I think customer service is really important to British Gas' competitiveness.' This is a conclusion, but it does not really demonstrate any deeper thinking on the issue.

One technique you can use when arriving at a conclusion is to use the phrase 'it depends'. For example, look at the following conclusion:

Student A:

In conclusion, customer service can be a very important source of competitiveness. However it is unlikely that you will need to use the customer service department at a gas company very often unless there is a gas leak or a mistake has been made with your bill. Therefore the price of the gas is much more likely to be important in increasing the competitiveness of British Gas than its level of customer service. The importance of customer service really depends on how often British Gas' customers need to use it and whether or not it is better than the customer service at rival gas companies.

> **Remember**
> In your conclusion make sure you show some original thinking. Don't simply repeat what you have already said. The 'it depends' rule will help you do this.

For each of the following conclusions, identify and explain one factor on which it will depend.

1. The most effective way for the business to improve its profitability is to reduce its costs.

   However, whether this is a success will depend on ....
   ....

   This is because ....
   ....

2. The most important element of the marketing mix is low prices. This is because, when consumer confidence is poor, having low prices will increase demand.

   However, the importance of low prices depends on ....
   ....

   This is because ....
   ....
   ....

> **Remember**
> Don't use 'it depends' only in your conclusion. You need to be thinking about this throughout your answer.

Activity 3: Improve an answer

Look at the answer below. It is a strong response, but it lacks a conclusion.
Your task is to write a suitable conclusion.

The response is based on the following question:

Assess the impact of using loans as a method of financing the growth of a business.

(8 marks)

Student A:

Loans give the business access to large amounts of capital which they can use to expand quickly. This will be important because, if the business has a competitive advantage, loans will give it the ability to expand faster than its competitors who might be relying on other sources of finance.

However, loans can be an expensive way to expand. This is because interest has to be paid on them and this will increase the business' costs. As a result, the business' costs will increase and this will cause profit to fall. If the expansion does not work, the business could also be at risk of failure if it cannot afford to meet its loan repayments.

In conclusion ....

....

....

....

....

....

....

....

....

....

....

....

....

Remember

Show some original thinking in your conclusion. Don't simply repeat what you have already said.

71

Activity 4: Write an answer

Look at the case study and question below:

> The Saltash Toy Box is a small independent retailer located in Cornwall. It cannot compete on price with larger retailers such as ToysRUs, but instead focuses on customer service and allowing children to play with toys, in store, before parents buy them.
>
> Despite its efforts to compete, however, sales at the store remained low. The owner decided to change the focus of the business. In 2010, the Saltash Toy Box closed its only retail store and instead decided to focus on catalogues and its website as a way of making sales. It believed this would boost the company's profits and increase the productivity of its two staff.
>
> *Assess the effects of the change of focus on the competitiveness of the Saltash Toy Box.*
>
> *(8 marks)*

Remember
When a question asks you to 'Assess' you must offer some balance.

You need to remember the following things when writing an answer to an 'Assess' question:

- You need to write up to **three** paragraphs.

- The first paragraph should explain one effect with up to **two** reasons/causes/consequences.

- The second paragraph should explain a second effect with up to **two** reasons/causes/consequences.

- The third paragraph should contain balance by attaching a value to the effects you have examined in the first two paragraphs. You should aim to make use of the 'it depends' rule.

- Your answer must be applied to the context.

 On a separate piece of paper write an answer to this question.
Give yourself no longer than 8 minutes to do this.

You or a friend can now mark the answer using the mark scheme on page 93.

Activity 1: Understanding the exam question

'Assess' questions need you to show **balance** and/or place a value on points you make. For each of the questions below you are provided with an argument. Provide an opposing argument for each one and place a value on the argument.

Question 1:

Assess the effect of lower interest rates on the UK economy. (8 marks)

Remember

A good way of showing balance is to begin a paragraph with 'however'.

Argument	Balancing argument
Lower interest rates might mean that consumers spend more of their income. This is because mortgage repayments will be lower and they will have more disposable income. This will benefit businesses in the economy as they are likely to receive higher sales. In the longer term this may cause economic growth.	*However,* .... *But this depends on* ....

Question 2:

Businesses such as Microsoft and Sky can be described as monopolies.

Assess the impact of monopolies on consumers in the UK. (8 marks)

Argument	Balancing argument
Monopolies can be harmful for consumers. By having no real competition, Sky can charge very high prices for films and sport channels. Consumers have to pay these prices as there are no alternative companies providing these channels. The size of the effect on consumers does depend on how strong the monopoly is – people do not HAVE to buy Sky, for example.	*However,* .... *But this depends on* ....

Activity 2: How do I use the 'it depends' rule?

In the previous activity we looked at how to bring balance into an answer. In this activity we are going to look at another important aspect of meeting the command word 'assess' or 'evaluate' and that is the use of the 'it depends' rule.

To answer the question, you will need to arrive at a clear conclusion. However, it is not enough to simply repeat what you have already said. For example: 'In conclusion, I think cash flow is an important reason for business failure.' This is a conclusion, but does not really demonstrate any deeper thinking.

One technique you can use when arriving at a conclusion is to use the phrase 'it depends'. For example, look at the following conclusion:

In conclusion, cash flow can be an important cause of business failure. This is especially true if the business has poor cash flow over a long period of time. If it is only a short-term issue, then the business can probably borrow money from the bank using an overdraft to get over the problem. The extent to which cash flow might cause the failure of the business therefore depends on how long the problem lasts for.

> **Remember**
> In your conclusion make sure you show some original thinking. Don't simply repeat what you have already said. 'It depends' will help you do this.

For each of the following, identify and explain one factor on which it will depend.

1. The most effective way for the government to reduce relative poverty in the UK is to increase state benefits.

   However, whether this is a success will depend on ....

   This is because ....

   ....

2. Whether high levels of economic growth will be good for the economy depends on

   ....

   This is because ....

   ....

3. Increasing price is one important way in which a business could increase profits.

   However, whether this works or not will depend on ....

   ....

   This is because ....

   ....

   ....

> **Remember**
> Don't use 'it depends' only in your conclusion. You need to be thinking about this throughout your answer.

Activity 3: Improve an answer

Look at the student response below. It is a strong response, but it lacks a conclusion. Your task is to write a suitable conclusion for this response.

The response below is based on the following question:

> *Assess the impact of a rise in interest rates on UK consumers.* *(8 marks)*

Student A:

Higher interest rates will mean that consumers have less money to spend. This is because mortgage payments will increase and so they will be left with less disposable income. Higher interest rates will therefore be bad for consumers.

On the other hand, if a consumer has savings, higher interest rates will be a good thing. This will mean they have more income and can increase their spending. As a result, their standard of living should increase.

In conclusion ....
....
....
....
....
....
....
....
....
....
....
....
....

....

....

Remember

Show some original thinking in your conclusion. Don't simply repeat what you have already said.

Activity 4: Write an answer

Look at the question below:

Assess the view that profit is the best way to measure the success of a business.

(8 marks)

Remember

When a question asks you to 'Assess', you must offer some balance.

Use the following checklist to help you plan your response.

Checklist	Tick
I have spent about 8 minutes writing my answer.	
I have made a decision about the extent to which profit is the best measure of success.	
I have written a developed paragraph on why profit is a good measure of success. I have given at least one reason/cause/consequence.	
I have written a developed paragraph on other possible measures of success and have given at least one reason/cause/consequence why these other measures might be an effective measure of success.	
I have attached a value to the measures I have identified – I have said how important they are and why.	
I have used the 'it depends' rule – for example, which measure is dependent on how the business defines 'success'.	
My answer uses the context given where appropriate.	
I have written a conclusion which does not just re-state the question.	

 On a separate piece of paper write an answer to this question.
Give yourself no longer than 8 minutes to do this.

You or a friend can now mark the answer using the mark scheme on page 94.

Introduction to 'Using your knowledge of economics/business, assess...' questions

The **final question** on the exam paper will usually start with the phrase 'Using your knowledge of economics/business, assess...' The question will be linked to a case study at the start of Section C and will be worth 10 marks.

Most questions refer to a particular issue faced by a business or an economy. To answer the question you have to judge how important that issue is compared with at least **one** other issue. You must write in context throughout your answer.

It is a good idea to write using up to **four** paragraphs.

- The first paragraph will explain why the issue highlighted is important.
- The second paragraph will explain why a different issue is more or less important.
- The third paragraph will explain why a third issue is more or less important.
- The final paragraph should contain a judgement as to which issue is the most important and why.

You might also make use of the 'it depends' rule. This is where the importance of one of the problems/benefits/opportunities changes depending on certain circumstances, e.g. the importance of having low prices will be greater if the UK economy enters a recession, so the effectiveness of low prices will depend on the economic situation.

A student aiming for the top grades should try to score at least 8 marks on this type of question.

> **Hint**
>
> Try to ensure that your answer is written in context and contains the phrase 'it depends'. This will help your answer to be placed in the top level of the mark scheme.

A typical question

Using your knowledge of business, assess the importance of good communication to a company such as Affinity. (10 marks)

A 10-mark answer

Good communication is essential to a small company like Affinity. It has grown by producing high quality guide books that meet the needs of families with small children. Without good communication, mistakes are occurring in its books and this is reducing the strength of Affinity's brand and reducing the amount of sales and profit it makes. This could damage Affinity's ability to grow in the future.

However, good communication is only one factor which should be important to Affinity. The quality of the guide books is arguably much more important. This is because any problems with poor communication should be noticed by the quality control department before the book is published. Without a good quality book, especially if it is being used as a guide or map, consumers will not purchase — reducing the number of sales Affinity makes.

Low prices are also important to Affinity since, without them, families will be put off from buying the book. This will reduce the amount of books that are sold and leave Affinity with large stocks, which it will have difficulty in selling in winter when the weather turns bad.

Good communication is important to Affinity, but it is only one of many things that will allow the company to be a success. Arguably having a good product is more important and, although poor communication can affect this, a quality control department should be able to prevent any problems from poor communication affecting the final guide books. The extent to which communication is important is dependent on the degree to which the final guide book is checked before being released to market.

Why does this response gain 10 marks?

Like other extended writing questions, the final question is assessed using a 'levels of response' mark scheme. The top level of the mark scheme (8–10 marks) can be seen below:

Level	Descriptor
Level 3 8-10 marks	Candidates consider the importance of communication to Affinity and offer **two or more** reasons/causes/consequences, etc. in support.
	At the lower end of the level some value will be attached to these reasons whilst at the top of the level there will be clear recognition of the value of the points made to the business, identifying an advantage and disadvantage, cost/benefit, pro/con, etc. or using the 'it depends' rule. At this level candidates are likely to offer at least one other factor to balance out the answer.
	At the middle of the level a judgement/conclusion will be made with some support drawn from the analysis.
	At the top of the level a judgement/conclusion will be given, clearly drawn from the analysis, representing a coherent argument, and will refer to the context.

The sample answer scored 10 marks (top level 3) because there was a four-paragraph answer. The first paragraph explains **two** reasons why good communication is important and the next two paragraphs explain why two other factors might be more important than good communication. The final paragraph makes a judgement as to the degree to which good communication is important, using the 'it depends' rule. Throughout the answer the Affinity context is used.

Activity 1: Understanding the exam question

Look at the case study evidence and question below:

> In 2008 Pepsi launched its first major product since 1993. Pepsi Raw is a cola drink that is made entirely from natural ingredients, and contains no artificial flavouring or sweeteners. Critics of the new drink argue that Pepsi is using the words 'raw' and 'natural' to make consumers believe that the new cola is a healthy product. Although each bottle contains 25% fewer calories than regular Pepsi-Cola, it still contains more calories and high levels of sugar compared with other healthier drinks.
>
> *Using your knowledge of business, assess whether Pepsi is right to use the words 'raw' and 'natural' in relation to its new product.*　　　　　(10 marks)

Think of four reasons why Pepsi might be right/wrong in using the words 'raw' and 'natural' to describe its new cola. Place these reasons in the left hand column of the table below. Then in the right hand column think of an opposing statement that will allow you to evaluate and demonstrate balance. Reason A and its balancing statement have been completed for you.

Place each of the four reasons in order of importance (1 = least important, 4 = most important).

	Reasons why Pepsi might be right/wrong	Balancing statement	Importance
A	There is nothing illegal in using the words 'natural' and 'raw'. (right)	*It might not be illegal but if it is not totally true it could be seen as being unethical, since they imply a healthy product.*	
B			
C			
D			

Thinking of four reasons/balancing statements and then placing them in order will give you the basic structure of how to approach the question. You can then pick three of those reasons and develop them in each of the first three paragraphs. In the conclusion you can then attach an importance to the reasons and explain which argument is the most powerful.

This is not dissimilar to the structure you may have used when completing your controlled assessment task!

Activity 2: Using the mark scheme

Look at the case study and question below:

In 2010 Marks and Spencer launched a brand new shirt called FreshMax. The shirt uses technology originally developed for football shirts and is designed to prevent embarrassing sweat patches appearing in hot weather, helping the wearer to stay looking cool and 'sweat free'. The shirts are priced at £50 and are more than twice the price of a normal Marks and Spencer shirt.

Marks and Spencer hopes that innovations such as the FreshMax shirt will help it to compete against supermarkets like Asda and Tesco who sell cheap clothing. Asda can sell a basic man's shirt for as little as £6, 88% cheaper than the Marks and Spencer FreshMax.

Using your knowledge of business, assess the extent to which innovation will allow Marks and Spencer to increase its profitability. (10 marks)

Now look at the mark scheme for this question below:

Level	Descriptor
Level 3 8-10 marks	Candidates consider the importance of innovation in allowing Marks and Spencer to increase its profits and offer **two or more** reasons/causes/consequences, etc. in support.
	At the lower end of the level some value will be attached to these reasons whilst at the top of the level there will be clear recognition of the value of the points made to the business, identifying an advantage and disadvantage, cost/benefit, pro/con, etc. or using the 'it depends' rule. At this level candidates are likely to offer at least one other factor to balance out the answer.
	At the middle of the level a judgement/conclusion will be made with some support drawn from the analysis.
	At the top of the level a judgement/conclusion will be given, clearly drawn from the analysis, representing a coherent argument and referring to the context.

Use the mark scheme above to mark Student A's answer below. Place your mark in the box below the answer (which continues on the next page).

Student A:

Innovation will be important to Marks and Spencer. Marks and Spencer target different consumers to supermarkets such as Asda. As a result, the quality of the product is much more important and innovation helps Marks and Spencer's clothes to stand out, giving them a unique selling point. Shirts like the FreshMax are attractive to high income consumers like businessmen, who do not want to look sweaty for an important meeting. These people are likely to pay £50 for a shirt despite cheaper shirts being available in supermarkets. This is because businessmen will not view an Asda shirt as being anywhere near as good as the Marks and Spencer FreshMax. Therefore Marks and Spencer will sell a lot of these shirts despite the high price, because there is nothing as good on the market – boosting Marks and Spencer's profitability.

However, innovation is very expensive and time consuming. As a result, introducing the FreshMax will increase Marks and Spencer's costs. Therefore, unless Marks and Spencer sell lots of shirts it is possible that Marks and Spencer's profits will fall.

Innovation is also only one part of why consumers shop at Marks and Spencer. Factors such as customer service and value for money are also important in boosting the profitability of the company.

Although innovation is important to Marks and Spencer, it is possible that innovation could cause profitability to go down rather than up.

Mark awarded = [/10]

In the space below, justify your mark and suggest any possible improvements:

Justification for mark awarded:

....
....
....
....
....
....
....

Possible improvements:

....
....
....
....
....
....
....

Activity 3: Write an answer

Look at the case study and question below:

Megabus is a discount bus company owned by Stagecoach plc. The business offers a 'no-frills' bus service between towns and cities in the UK. To travel on a Megabus, customers have to book in advance on the Internet. After making the booking, Megabus sends a text message to the customer's mobile phone and the customer shows this to the driver on boarding the bus. Technology like this allows Megabus to keep its costs down. Lower costs also allow Megabus to offer very low fares; Manchester to London can be as cheap as £5 if booked early enough.

However, some customers have criticised the overall service provided by Megabus. The buses can be old and the on-board facilities poor – the toilet can often be blocked, for example. Breakdowns have also occurred and passengers have complained about a lack of legroom. Some passengers want Megabus to improve the quality of its service.

Using your knowledge of business, evaluate which element of the marketing mix is most likely to improve Megabus' ticket sales. **(10 marks)**

You need to remember the following things when writing an answer to this question:

○ You need to write up to **four** paragraphs.

○ The first paragraph should explain why one element of the marketing mix could be important in allowing Megabus to improve its ticket sales.

○ The second paragraph should explain why a different element of the marketing mix may be important in allowing Megabus to improve its ticket sales.

○ The third paragraph should explain why a third element of the marketing mix may be important in allowing Megabus to improve its ticket sales.

○ In the final paragraph you need to make a judgement as to which element of the marketing mix you have considered in the first three paragraphs is the most important in allowing Megabus to increase sales of tickets, explaining why.

○ Use the 'it depends' rule, since different elements of the marketing mix may be more important in different situations, e.g. if there are lots of other rival bus/train competitors.

○ Your answer must be applied to the context, i.e. Megabus.

 On a separate piece of paper write an answer to this question. Give yourself no longer than 10 minutes to do this. It would be a good idea to divide this time up into 2½ minutes for each of the four paragraphs.

You or a friend can now mark the answer using the mark scheme on page 95.

Activity 1: Understanding the exam question

Look at the case study evidence and question below:

Bebo acquired by AOL

The social networking business, Bebo, has been acquired by media giant AOL in a takeover deal worth £417 million. AOL is part of the Time Warner group. Bebo was set up by husband and wife duo Michael and Xochi Birch in 2005. The couple will get several hundred million dollars from the takeover deal. AOL say that they think that the large user base of Bebo will help them make more money in the future from selling advertising on Bebo and they see it as a good deal.

Others are not quite so sure. Social networking sites like Bebo, MySpace and DoubleClick are being swallowed up by large media corporations and some have questioned whether they will retain their roots.

Using the evidence and your knowledge of economics and business, assess the extent to which consumers of social networking sites, and employees of a business like Bebo, will be disadvantaged by the takeover. (10 marks)

Think of two ways in which consumers and two ways in which employees will be disadvantaged by the takeover. Place these in the left hand column of the table below. In the right hand column think of an opposing statement that will allow you to evaluate and demonstrate balance. Reason A has been completed for you.

Now place each of the four impacts in order of importance in the final column (1 = least important, 4 = most important).

Disadvantages for consumers		Balancing statement	Importance
A	Less competition will mean choice is restricted for consumers.	*AOL is a powerful company and may well invest in the Bebo site and make it even better.*	
B			

Disadvantages for employees		Balancing statement	Importance
C			
D			

Thinking of four reasons/balancing statements and then placing them in order will give you the basic structure of how to approach the question. You can then pick three of those reasons and develop them in each of the first three paragraphs. In the conclusion you can then attach an importance to the reasons and explain which argument is the most powerful.

This is not dissimilar to the structure you may have used when completing your controlled assessment task!

Activity 2: Using the mark scheme

Look at the case study and question below:

In recent years China has enjoyed record levels of economic growth. However, in this race for growth, the Chinese government has been accused of sacrificing the environment so as to benefit from rapid economic development.

In one town, clouds of yellow smoke hang in the air as a result of the constant burning of plastic. The workers suffer from the polluted fumes from the fires which melt the plastic. The cause of this pollution is the burning of supermarket bags and food packaging waste, imported from Britain. Pollution of this kind not only affects people living in the area, it can also have lasting effects which can affect future generations.

The Chinese government is under increased pressure to regulate pollution in order to achieve sustainable growth.

Economic growth can lead to problems such as pollution. Using your knowledge of business and economics, assess the case for the Chinese government using regulation to achieve sustainable economic growth. (10 marks)

Now look at the mark scheme for this question:

Level	Descriptor
Level 3 8-10 marks	In this level the candidate will have identified **at least two** reasons why governments such as China should impose regulation upon the growth of firms. In this level there will be clear recognition of the value of the points made to China, identifying an advantage and disadvantage, cost/benefit, pro/con, etc. or using the 'it depends' rule. At this level candidates are likely to offer at least one other factor to balance out the answer and attach more value to the points being made.
	At the middle of the level a judgement/conclusion will be made with some support drawn from the analysis.
	At the top of the level a judgement/conclusion will be clearly drawn from the analysis, representing a coherent argument and referring to the context.
	Responses will have a clear evaluative slant and will recognise that one perspective might be stronger than the other. Expect some candidates to refer to potential drawbacks to regulation and the ability of governments to police it. The answer will be articulated using business terminology and will show the candidate has clearly understood what the command word 'assess' means.

Use the mark scheme to mark Student A's answer below. Place your mark in the box below the answer.

Student A:

Sustainable economic growth does not cause damage to the environment so that future generations are not impacted negatively. Regulation is an important way that China could achieve this type of growth. Regulation is rules and restrictions placed on business. China may regulate the amount of pollution that businesses are allowed to make. This will therefore reduce the amount of pollution and should bring down the negative externalities that people suffer as a result of business activity. Also, regulation will mean that businesses have to pay for the damage they cause.

However, regulation may not work. It can be argued that it is consumers who should pay the price for environmental damage, as they create the demand. Imposing rules and restrictions on businesses will do nothing to reduce this demand. Also, regulation will mean that businesses may move to countries where rules are more relaxed.

Regulation is also only one way in which sustainable economic growth can be encouraged. However, it is unlikely, in itself, to achieve sustainable economic growth. It depends on how far-reaching the regulation is. If China completely banned the use of coal in its industry, then this would have a major impact. However, it is unlikely to be so severe in its rules.

Mark awarded = [   ] /10

In the space below, justify your mark and suggest any possible improvements:

Justification for mark awarded:

....

....

....

....

....

Possible improvements:

....

....

....

....

....

....

Activity 3: Write an answer

Look at the case study and question below:

Greggs plc, the bakers, originated in the North East of England in 1984. It has grown through internal and external means. Greggs has expanded to the rest of the country by taking over other regional bakery chains. By 1994 it had 502 shops across the UK. In 1994 it took over a rival business, Bakers Oven, adding an extra 424 shops.

Greggs wanted the Bakers Oven format because many of its shops had in-store bakeries. Greggs had large central bakeries which delivered its products to local shops.

Year	2004	2005	2006	2007	2008
Operating profit (£m)	44.7	47.1	42.2	47.7	44.3

*Using the evidence and your knowledge of economics and business, assess the extent to which customers **and** shareholders might benefit from the growth of Greggs plc.*

(10 marks)

You need to remember the following things when writing an answer to this question:

○ You need to write at least **three** paragraphs. For this question it seems sensible to use a three rather than four paragraph approach.

○ The first paragraph should explain two ways in which one group will benefit.

○ The second paragraph should explain two ways in which the other group will be affected.

○ The third paragraph should explain why different groups may be affected in different ways.

○ The final paragraph allows you to make a judgement as to which group is most affected. Use the 'it depends' rule, since customers and shareholders are likely to be affected differently.

○ Your answer must be applied clearly to the context, i.e. Greggs plc.

 On a separate piece of paper write an answer to this question. Give yourself no longer than 10 minutes to do this.

You or a friend can now mark the answer using the mark scheme on page 96.

Remember
Be original in your conclusion. Don't simply repeat what you have already said.

Page 7
Activity 1: Understanding the exam question
A Good. B Bad. C Bad. D Bad. E Answer. F Bad.

Activity 2: Build an answer
Salary = a fixed payment per year which is paid monthly.

Page 8
Activity 1: Understanding the exam question
A Bad. B Good. C Good. D Bad. E Answer. F Good.

Activity 2: Build an answer
Economies of scale = where average total costs fall when output increases.

Page 10
Activity 1: Using the mark scheme
Student A = 2 marks.
1. advertising   2 offer money-off vouchers

Student B = 2 marks.

You do not have to write a lot to gain both of the marks. Take careful note of the command words as your guide to what the answer requires. By writing several full sentences, you are reducing the amount of time you have for the longer questions later on in the exam. Student A used 56 words and Student B 6 words – both got the same marks!

Page 11
Activity 1: Using the mark scheme
Student A = 2 marks.
1. making more money (profit)
2. to increase market share

Student B = 2 marks.

You do not have to write a lot to gain both of the marks. Take careful note of the command words as your guide to what the answer requires. By writing several full sentences, you are reducing the amount of time you have for the longer questions later on in the exam. Student A used 55 words and Student B 5 words – both got the same marks!

Page 13
Activity 1: Build an answer
Student A = 1 mark. This is because the answer made a simple point about 'ethics' involving doing the right thing. To raise the answer to 2 marks, the student could have added a second sentence that included an example, e.g. *'The Co-op tries to do the right thing because its plastic bags biodegrade and it sells lots of FairTrade products'.*

Page 14
Activity 1: Build an answer
Student A = 1 mark. This is because the answer made a simple point about 'exchange rate' involving the value of a currency. To raise the answer to 2 marks, the student could have added a second sentence that included an example, e.g. *'The exchange rate is how much a currency is worth. For example, £1 will currently buy $1.65 – this is its exchange rate'.*

Page 16
Activity 1: Understanding the exam question
1. 5 paddling pools.

2. 75 – 5 = 70 paddling pools.

3. Day 8 – Day 3 = 5 days.

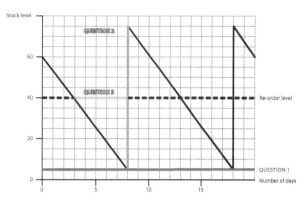

Page 18
Activity 1: Understanding the exam question
2007(12)–2008(9)
Inflation speeds up from 2% to over 5%. Lower interest rates which lead to higher consumer spending. This is because loans become more expensive and spending on goods such as cars falls with higher rates.

2008(9)–2009(7)
Inflation slows from over 5% to just under 2%. One reason could be the increase in interest rates by the Bank of England. This causes households to have less disposable income due to higher mortgage payments. Pressure on prices therefore falls.

Page 19
Activity 2: Understanding the exam question
A 0 marks. No real understanding.
B 2 marks. Clear definition and example drawn from the diagram.
C 1 mark. Knows what is meant by the exchange rate, but does not use an example from the chart.

Page 21
Activity 1: Using the mark scheme
Student A = 2 marks. This is because there is no formula stated and this is asked for in the question. The student has calculated contribution per unit, therefore evidence of 'workings' exists and they have provided the correct answer. The answer could be improved by providing a formula because that has been asked for in the question.

Page 22
Activity 2: Build an answer
Formula: Profit = Total revenue – Total costs
Numbers into formula: Revenue: 20,000 consoles x £300 = £6,000,000
Total costs: £2,400,000 (fixed costs) + (£140 x 20,000) (variable costs) = £5,200,000
Answer in correct units: £6,000,000 – £5,200,000 = £800,000.

Page 23
Activity 1: Build an answer
The business should charge the higher price. Customers for this business are clearly price insensitive. This is because revenue when price is low is £200,000, but when price is increased, revenue increases to £225,000. This shows that customers will still buy the product even when it goes up in price. This shows price insensitivity.

Page 24
Activity 2: Build an answer
Calculate amount: €5/1.25 = £4
Multiply the unit price by number of units: £4 x 100 = 400
Answer in correct currency: £400

Page 26
Activity 1: Using the mark scheme
Student A = 1 mark. Response gives a list and does not provide development of either point. A list, as long as it includes valid suggestions, scores 1 mark. Both of the consumer protection laws listed are valid.

Student B = 2 marks. The response offers a valid suggestion – the Trades Description Act – and provides an example developing the answer.

Page 27
Activity 2: Understanding the question
A Not. These are two separate points. The second sentence does not develop the first. This answer scores 1 mark since both sentences are independent of one another.
B Developed. The point is made and then linked to a second point. The second point then leads into a third linked point. The overall result is 3 marks.
C Developed. The point of increasing costs is given and then two separate unlinked reasons are given as to why costs might increase. The answer scores 2 marks.

Page 28
Activity 3: Improve an answer
Student A:
A No. Definitions are not required in 'Outline' questions.
B No. The answer already has one link between sentence 2 and sentence 3.
C No. Paragraphs are not needed in a 2-mark answer.
D No. This is a 2-mark 'Outline' question. There is no need for lots of detail.
E Yes. The candidate has provided two points and developed one. The first sentence was unnecessary.

Student B:
A No. The student already does this.
B No. Paragraphs are not needed in a 2-mark answer.
C No. This is a 2-mark 'Outline' question. There is no need for lots of detail.
D Yes. There are two linked sentences. For a 2-mark answer only one is necessary.

Page 29
Activity 1: Using the mark scheme
Student A = 1 mark. Response provides a list and does not 'outline' any of the reasons. A list, providing it includes valid suggestions, scores 1 mark. Several of the suggestions – lower interest rates and investment – are acceptable.

Student B = 2 marks. The response offers a valid suggestion and provides some development of this. Sentences are used to build a coherent explanation.

Page 30
Activity 2: Understanding the question
A Not. Uses 'also' to introduce another problem.
B Developed. Response uses the phrase 'This will mean..'
C Not. Response provides balance rather than a development of the point.

Page 31
Activity 3: Improve an answer
Student A:
A Yes. Definitions are not rewarded in 'Outline' questions.
B No. The response already includes linked statements.
C No. Paragraphs are not necessary in this type of question.
D No. This is a 3-mark 'Outline' question. There is no need for

lots of details.
E Yes. This will ensure all of the 3 marks.

Student B:
A No. Student already does this.
B No. Paragraphs are not necessary in this type of question.
C No. This is a 2-mark 'Outline' question. There is no need for lots of details.
D No. Student already does this.

Page 33
Activity 1: Using the mark scheme
Student A = 2 marks. There is a point made about 'differentiation allowing the product to stand out in the market' and this is developed. The student states that this is because the product is now 'seen as being different'. However, there is no use of the Subway context at all. Since the name Subway appears in the question, a 3-mark answer must be applied to the business. The answer could be improved by having a clear sandwich/Subway use of context.

Page 34
Activity 2: Improve an answer
Subway's baguettes   sandwich/fast food market
sandwiches/baguettes   Pret a Manger   healthy sandwiches

Page 35
Activity 3: Write an answer
Question 1 does not mention the name of a business. Therefore 3 marks can be gained by writing up to three unrelated sentences as to how improved worker motivation might benefit a business or two points with some development of one of them.

Question 2 does mention the name of a business, so without clear reference to Apple or its products or competition, a student will not be able to gain full marks.

Page 36
Activity 1: Using the mark scheme
Student A = 2 marks. A point is made – 'diseconomies of scale' – and some development is provided about the business being more difficult to manage. The point that 'costs will rise' is not accepted. The student should have referred to average costs. The answer could have been improved by making another point and developing this.

Page 37
Activity 2: Improve an answer
bad   more expensive   benefit   cheaper

Page 38
Activity 3: Write an answer
Question 1 does not mention the name of a business. Therefore 3 marks can be gained by writing up to three unrelated sentences as to how low interest rates might benefit a business or two points with some development of one of them. Question 2 does mention the name of a business, so without clear reference to McDonald's and its products or competition, a student will not be able to gain full marks.

Page 40
Activity 1: Understanding the exam question
State benefit: Reduces the amount of refrigerated space McDonald's needs to store burgers/meat etc., because…
1st sentence: Stocks of meat and burgers will be arriving just before McDonald's runs out. As a result…
2nd sentence: McDonald's costs will fall because their restaurants can be smaller, using less land.

Page 41
Activity 2: Using the mark scheme
Student A = 2 marks. This is because a statement is made that strong cash flow prevents Lidl running out of cash. This is then linked to Lidl being able to 'pay its suppliers on time'. The definition at the start of the answer does not generate any extra marks because this question is asking you to 'explain'. To move to 3 marks, the answer needs more use of context. Although Lidl has been mentioned, it is possible to replace the word Lidl with any other company and the answer would still 'work'. Perhaps the word 'suppliers' could be replaced with 'farmers'/'food manufacturers'.

Page 42
Activity 3: Improve an answer
This results in *Co-operative Food being more attractive to consumers who care about ethical issues and the environment*. As a result Co-operative Food can *increase the prices of its groceries, since demand will become more price insensitive compared to supermarkets like Asda*.

Page 43
Activity 1: Understanding the exam question
State benefit: Economies of scale will result in a fall in the average costs of the firm.
1st sentence: This will enable them to reduce the selling price of its product/service.
2nd sentence: which will give it an advantage over its rivals.

Page 44
Activity 2: Using the mark scheme
Student A = 2 marks. This is because the statement is made that trade restrictions will help to maintain employment (1 mark) and that this will lead to higher standard of living (1 mark). There is a clear link between the two statements; this is necessary for an 'Explain' question. The definition at the start of the answer does not generate any extra marks because this question is asking you to 'explain'. To move to 3 marks, the answer needs an additional linking statement. For example, the student could have said that employment would have been increased because customers would be unable to buy foreign imports, and that this would lead to higher incomes and living standards.

Page 45
Activity 3: Improve an answer
This may mean that *its profit margin is reduced*. Because of *this the business may have to increase prices it charges its customers*.

Page 48
Activity 1: Understanding the exam question
A5, B3, C4, D2
Answers below are dependent on a person's opinion, but expect low prices and low waiting time to be the most important.
A Productivity, B Quality of product, C Productivity, D Quality of product

Page 49
Activity 2: Using the mark scheme
Student A = 5 marks. The student has written three paragraphs which is a good structure to use. Increased quality has been developed and there are at least two reasons/causes/consequences. This is then repeated in the second paragraph when productivity is developed. The final paragraph contains a conclusion where a choice is made and some support is given, but there is a general lack of McDonald's/fast food context preventing 6 marks being awarded.

Page 50
Activity 3: Improve an answer
A Weak. Although there were references to McDonald's, the word McDonald's could have been removed and another non-food business could be inserted and the answer would still make sense.
B Strong. Three paragraphs are offered.
C Strong. Lots of good business language is used.
D Strong. Each paragraph contained at least two reasons/causes/consequences.

Student B:
By improving the quality of its product McDonald's can stand out compared to rival fast food companies such as Burger King and KFC. This will allow it to sell more burgers and gain a strong brand image. If its image is strong it can charge more for its burgers and make larger profits making McDonald's more competitive.

Productivity is how many burgers McDonald's can make in a period of time. If McDonald's makes more burgers in an hour, the wages paid to its staff will be divided up over more units of output. As a result the average cost of each burger will be reduced, giving McDonald's a greater profit margin on each burger sold.

As a result, improving productivity is the most important factor in improving McDonald's competitiveness because McDonald's focus on fast food which is aimed at consumers who want to buy food in a hurry. Since the prices paid are quite low consumers are not really looking for high quality food and really want their food much more quickly. Improving productivity allows this to happen.

Student A:
By improving the quality of its product McDonald's can stand out compared to other firms. This will allow it to sell more of its products and gain a strong brand image. If its image is strong it can charge more for its goods and services and make larger profits, making the firm more competitive.

Productivity is how many goods and services a firm can make in a period of time. If McDonalds makes more of its product in an hour, the wages paid to its staff will be divided up over more units of output. As a result the average cost of each item will be reduced, giving McDonalds a greater profit margin on each item sold.

As a result, improving productivity is most important because it allows profits to be increased much more quickly.

(Yellow highlighting = use of context.)

Page 51
Activity 4: Build an answer
Paragraph 1: *By only selling fruit grown in the UK, Tesco would become more appealing to customers who care about the environment.*
Reason/cause/consequence 1: T*his is because the fruit will not need to be shipped as far, reducing the amount of food miles. This will lead to less carbon dioxide being released into the atmosphere.*
Reason/cause/consequence 2: *If this is attractive to Tesco's customers they will have the opportunity to raise prices on its British fruit and make a larger profit.*

Paragraph 2: *Tesco could do nothing because some fruit cannot be grown in the UK very easily without using heated greenhouses.*

Reason 1: *By continuing to sell fruit from Africa, Tesco will be able to sell a full range of fruit including pineapples and mangos.*

Reason 2: *This will give Tesco's customers more choice, making it less likely that they switch to rival supermarkets such as Sainsbury's.*

Decision: *Doing nothing is the best option for Tesco. If they only sell fruit grown in the UK, they will restrict the choice of fruit that the consumer has. This will cause customers to go to other supermarkets who will simply place larger orders for African fruit. Therefore pollution will not go down.*

Page 52
Activity 1: Understanding the exam question
A No. First sentence is a definition, followed by a consideration of an effect.
B Linked. Explains the effect of the lower interest rate on a lorry business (context), and then develops this further by suggesting how the business may respond to this change.
C No. The first sentence refers to businesses, but the second sentence, using the word 'also', goes on to consider the effect upon customers. No attempt to link these two points.

Page 53
Activity 2: Using the mark scheme
Student A = 5 marks. This response is awarded 5 marks. The response explains how both ways will help these businesses. Linked statements are provided as part of the explanations. Appropriate business terms and concepts are used. However, no conclusion is provided to make clear which is the best way. This was needed to gain full marks.

Page 54
Activity 3: Improve an answer
A Yes. The response is one continuous paragraph. It would have been better organised into paragraphs.
B Yes. This is a long response. It is not clear what the student's actual decision is. Make a judgement in the first few lines before going on to justify this.
C No. There are no marks awarded on this question for definitions.
D No. This response already contains lots of detail. In fact it contains too much. The student could have scored more marks by writing much less.
E No. Be bold and make a decision. Justify this decision with evidence and by demonstrating your knowledge of Business and Economics.

Pages 55–56
Activity 4: Build an answer
A …a fall in living standards in Kenya.
B …businesses will sell fewer goods and services to EU countries, due to tariffs which exist.
…it means there will be less economic growth in Kenya and
C The loss of revenue for businesses *will also* be a major impact for Kenya and its businesses.
D … it may mean that unemployment will rise. This may well cause government spending to increase.
… it means it cannot be spent elsewhere. This is an opportunity cost.
E The biggest impact will be on living standards. This is because the impact will be on stakeholders other than business owners. Everyone will suffer. The loss of revenue will mainly affect businesses. This is why living standards is the most important factor.

Page 59
Activity 1: Understanding the exam question
Possible benefits: Better quality of work; less absenteeism; greater worker loyalty; increased productivity; more creativity.

Page 60
Activity 2: Using the mark scheme
Student A = 6 marks. The three-paragraph structure makes it easy to mark. There are two developed reasons why promotion may/may not be important and the student has cleverly stated that the importance of motivation depends on the type of worker at KFC. The student has also written the answer in a clear KFC context. There is also reference to Maslow's hierarchy which is helpful and in context – not just a repeat of theory copied from a textbook. The only possible criticism is that the answer is longer than it needs to be to get 6 marks.

Page 61
Activity 3: Build an answer
Benefit 1: *One benefit of increased productivity is that the average total costs of making a car will go down.*
Reason/causes/consequences 1: *This means BMW will make a greater level of profit on each car sold.*
Reason/cause/consequence 2: *As a result, if BMW sells the same amount of cars, its total profits should increase.*

Benefit 2: *BMW will benefit from increased competitiveness.*
Reason/causes/consequences 1: *This is because lowering average total cost gives BMW the ability to lower prices.*
Reason/causes/consequences 2: *This will allow BMW to steal customers from rival car manufacturers such as Audi.*

Most important benefit: *Improving competitiveness is the most important benefit to BMW. This is because consumer confidence is low after the recession. Therefore consumers are more likely to purchase the car which offers them the best value for money.*

Page 63
Activity 1: Understanding the exam question
Possible disadvantages: high prices; low quality; poor customer service

Possible advantages: lower prices (due to economies of scale); innovation (stemming from high profits); natural monopoly

Page 64
Activity 2: Using the mark scheme
Student A = 5 marks. The three-paragraph structure makes it easy to mark. There are two developed reasons why promotion may be important and the student has cleverly recognised the importance of the competitive market that KFC operates in. The student has also written the answer in a clear KFC context. A mark is dropped for the final conclusion for not clearly stating whether promotion is the most appropriate strategy for KFC.

Page 65
Activity 3: Build an answer
Paragraph 1:
Benefit 1: One benefit of growing in size is that BMW will be able to buy components, like tyres and light bulbs, in bulk.
Reason/cause/consequence 1: This means it will be able to bring down its average costs of production.

Reason/cause/consequence 2: As a consequence of its lower average costs, BMW will be able to bring down its prices. This may make it more competitive against rivals such as Audi.

Paragraph 2:
Benefit 2: A second benefit is that BMW may become a monopoly (25% market share).
Reason/cause/consequence 1: *By controlling a major market share, businesses can become market leaders.*
Reason/cause/consequence 2: *As a result, it may be able to charge higher prices, as it has a stronger position than competitors.*

Most important benefit: *Bringing down average costs is most important for car producers at the current time.*
Reason: *This is because the market is very competitive and as a result of the recent recession people have less money to spend on luxuries like sports cars.*

Page 69
Activity 1: Understanding the exam question
Question 1: Balancing argument

However, *motivation does not have to go down. The remaining workers are the ones that have not lost their jobs and as a result they could be much more motivated to work for Sony and help make the company a success.*

But this depends on *whether or not the remaining employees think that they will lose their job in the future. If they don't it is likely that motivation will increase rather than fall.*

Question 2: Balancing argument

However, *it is likely that the value of the fringe benefits will be quite low compared to with the amount of salary or wage a worker is being paid. Therefore the extent to which fringe benefits will attract workers to First Great Western will be limited.*

But this depends on *the number of free rail tickets the worker gets. If the worker makes lots of long distance trips by rail, the value of the free rail tickets could be worth thousands of pounds. This will increase the number of people who want to work for First Great Western.*

Page 70
Activity 2: How do I use the 'it depends' rule?
1. However, whether this is a success will depend on *whether cutting costs will affect the quality of the product or service the business sells.*

   This is because *if the quality goes down, consumers will not be willing to pay as much for the product. As a result, revenue from the product could go down, which reduces rather than increases profit.*

2. However, the importance of low prices depends on *the kind of product the business is selling.*

   This is because *if the business is selling a luxury product such as a designer handbag, low prices will make consumers believe the handbag is cheap and of low quality. Therefore in this situation low prices are not an important element of the marketing mix.*

Page 71
Activity 3: Improve an answer
In conclusion *the impact of loans really depends on the amount borrowed and the interest rate charged by the bank. If the amount borrowed is low, the amount repayable with interest will be small so the impact on the business will be small.*

However, *if the company is expanding into a risky market it is likely that the business needs to borrow a large amount of money and if the bank thinks that there is a chance the business could fail, they will only lend if the interest rate is high. This will result in the business having to repay large sums of money which will reduce its profitability and cash flow and as a result the impact will be far greater.*

Page 73
Activity 1: Understanding the exam question
Question 1: Balancing argument
However, *if interest rates are too low then there is a chance that spending in the economy may increase too much. High levels of consumer spending can lead to higher inflation. This would be a real problem for the government, given its inflation target of 2%. But this depends on how low interest rates are and how much extra disposable income people have as a result.*

Question 2: Balancing argument
However, *as monopolies are big businesses they often have economies of scale (lower average costs). This means they can buy in bulk and charge customers low prices. Smaller businesses cannot do this. But this depends on whether the business passes on to consumers the lower average costs it enjoys. The high price of Sky packages suggests that this is not the case in this market.*

Page 74
Activity 2: How do I use the 'it depends' rule?
1. However, whether this is a success will depend on *how much state benefits increase by.*
   This is because *if benefits are too high people may choose not to work and therefore will find it harder to get out of poverty.*
2. Whether high levels of economic growth will be good for the economy depends on *how quickly the economy grows.*
   This is because if *economic growth is too high inflation may increase. This is a big priority for the government. It needs to get the right balance between growth and inflation.*
3. However, whether this works or not will depend on *how price sensitive its customers are.*
   This is because *if customers are very price sensitive, perhaps due to lots of competing businesses, then demand and revenue are likely to fall. This will therefore cause profits to fall.*

Page 75
Activity 3: Improve an answer
In conclusion, *the exact impact of a rise in interest rates depends on the circumstances of the individual. However, as most people have a mortgage, the overall impact on consumers will be negative and will negatively affect their standard of living.*

Pages 80-81
Activity 2: Using the mark scheme
Student A = 9 marks. The four-paragraph structure makes it easy to mark. The importance of innovation has been considered and a supported judgement has been made. A factor has been used to balance the answer since the candidate considers both the cost of innovation in paragraph 2 and the fact that customer service will also be important as well as innovation in paragraph 3. The answer is in context, but the conclusion could have been more sophisticated and perhaps made use of the 'it depends' rule. For instance, the level of competition in the clothing market means that innovation is essential in allowing Marks and Spencer to increase its profitability.

Pages 84–85
Activity 2: Using the mark scheme
Student A = 8 marks. The three-paragraph structure makes it easy to mark. The importance of regulation has been considered and

explained, and a supported judgement has been made. A factor has been used to balance the answer as the candidate considers the problems of regulation in paragraph 2. The answer is in context, but the conclusion could have been more sophisticated and perhaps made more use of the 'it depends' rule.

Mark schemes for diagram questions (p17)
Question 1:
Award 1 mark for evidence of workings and 1 mark for the correct answer. e.g. Actual output – Break-even level of output = Margin of safety 1,000 units – 750 units = 250 units.
Question 2:
Award 1 mark for evidence of workings and 1 mark for the correct answer. e.g. Total revenue – Total costs = Profit/loss £15,000 – £20,000 = £5,000 loss.

Mark schemes for 'Describe' questions (p35)
Question 1:
Indicative content

For 3 marks, the description will make three relevant points associated with improved worker motivation and how it might benefit a business or up to two points with some development of one of them. This may include a definition. Each descriptive strand will clearly show the importance of improved worker motivation to the business. One mark is awarded for the statement of a benefit, with 1 mark for each relevant point.

Possible benefits include:

• Higher levels of profit.

• Higher productivity.

• Improved customer service.

• Enhanced branding.

• Lower unit costs.

Question 2:
Indicative content

For 3 marks, the description will clearly show the importance of the brand to the success of Apple. Within the answer there will be at least two clearly identifiable strands of description with some development. The answer should be rooted in the Apple/electronics context. Two marks are awarded for each strand of description and 1 mark is awarded for the use of context. One strand can include a definition.

Possible answers include:

• Makes the firm stand out.

• Increases the number of repeat purchases.

• Enables the firm to add value.

• Allows the firm to charge higher prices without the loss of demand.

• Makes it harder for a new firm to set up in competition.

Mark schemes for 'Describe' questions (p38)
Question 1:
Indicative content

For 3 marks, the description will make three relevant points associated with low interest rates and how these might benefit a business or up to two points with some development of one of them. This may include a definition. Each descriptive strand will clearly show the importance of improved worker motivation to the business.

Possible benefits include:

• Lower fixed costs.

• Higher sales due to higher disposable income for consumers.

• Increased consumer confidence.

• Lower unit costs.

Question 2:
Indicative content

For 3 marks, the description will clearly show how a business like McDonald's might measure its success. Within the answer there will be at least two clearly identifiable strands of description with some development. The answer should be rooted in the McDonald's/fast food context. Two marks are awarded for each strand of description and 1 mark is awarded for the use of context. One strand can include a definition.

Possible answers include:

• Higher sales revenue.

• Increased profit.

• Higher market share.

• Social success – e.g. sponsorships in the local community.

Mark schemes for 'Discuss' questions (p62)
Indicative content

The aim here is for candidates to consider the importance of advertising in allowing Poundland to increase its profits. The question asks the candidate to 'discuss', so the candidate must develop some evidence of balance within their answer. This could take the form of considering the drawbacks and costs of advertising and the likely risks of failure/success. Equally the route to evaluation could be achieved by considering other factors which are perhaps more important in allowing profits to increase, e.g. lower prices/improved product range, etc. or that it might depend on what sort of advertising Poundland carried out. The answer should be in the context of a discount retailer such as Poundland.

Reasons why advertising could increase profits:

• Gain more customers.

• Increase market share.

• Improves the brand.

Reasons advertising may not increase profits:

• Expensive.

• Might not work.

• Other retailers may also advertise at the same time.

• There are other ways to increase profitability.

Level	Descriptor
No mark	Non-rewardable material.
Level 1 1-2 marks	One reason as to why advertising could increase Poundland's profits is given with some simple development or two reasons are given with no development of either. An alternative route to marks in this level is if just a simple judgement or value is given to one benefit

1 mark can be awarded for no support and 2 if some simple support is offered. The candidate explains one reason why advertising is/is not important using terminology and inter-linkage of ideas. Alternatively, the candidate could identify two reasons, but the explanation is weak. A candidate who only explains one benefit well cannot go beyond 2 marks. Expect to see no reference to Poundland and answers linked to a generic business will be in this range. Answers in this level will have demonstrated no evaluative qualities.

Level 2

3-4 marks

Reference to two reasons is given with some development of each. A judgement/point is given at the lower end of the level with some development/support, which includes at least one cause/consequence, etc. for each benefit.

At the top of the level this analysis will be relevant and linked to the judgement/point made and there may be some reference to the context. At the bottom end of this level the candidate will have explained two reasons why advertising is/is not important using terminology and inter-linkage of ideas. Without any evaluation evident candidates cannot score above 3 marks.

However, if evaluation is implied or is superficial/ weak, e.g. 'advertising might not work', the candidate can reach the top of this level.

Level 3

5-6 marks

Reference to two benefits is given with development of each. A judgement/point is given with some development which includes at least two causes/consequences, etc. for each reason and may include some comparison between the two.

Answers at the top of this level will refer to the Poundland context. In this level there will be clear evaluation and the candidate will have discussed the importance of advertising new products in allowing Poundland to improve its profitability. Candidates in this level are likely to weigh advertising against other factors such as lower prices, product choice, etc. Answers in this level are likely to refer specifically to Poundland and the kinds of product it sells rather than a generic business.

Mark schemes for 'Discuss' questions (p66)
Indicative content

The aim here is for candidates to consider the importance of taxation in addressing the problem of binge drinking. The question asks the candidate to 'discuss', so the candidate must develop some evidence of balance within their answer. This could take the form of considering the drawbacks and costs of taxation and the likely risks of failure/success. Equally the route to evaluation could be achieved by considering other factors which are perhaps more important in dealing with the problem, such as regulation and education. The answer should be in the context of binge drinking.

Reasons why taxation might be effective:

• Will make alcohol more expensive.

• Young people have low levels of income.

• Alternative drinks will become relatively cheaper.

Reasons taxation may not be effective:

• Alcohol consumption is not price sensitive.

• Young people will always find a way to purchase alcohol.

• Education is more important.

Level	Descriptor
No mark	Non-rewardable material.
Level 1 1-2 marks	One reason as to why taxation might work is given with some simple development or two reasons are given with no development of either.
	An alternative route to marks in this level is if just a simple judgement or value is given to one benefit. 1 mark can be awarded for no support and 2 if some simple support is offered.
Level 2 3-4 marks	Reference to two reasons is given with some development of each. A judgement/point is given at the lower end of the level with some development/support, which includes at least one cause/consequence, etc. for each benefit.
	At the top of the level this analysis will be relevant and linked to the judgement/point made and there may be some reference to the context.
Level 3 5-6 marks	Reference to two benefits is given with development of each. A judgement/point is given with some development which includes at least two causes/consequences, etc. for each reason and may include some comparison between the two.
	Answers at the top of this level will refer to the alcohol context.

Mark schemes for 'Assess' questions (p72)
Indicative content

The aim here is for candidates to consider whether changing the 'place' element of the marketing mix will improve Saltash Toy Box's competitiveness. The question asks the candidate to 'assess', so the candidate must develop some evidence of balance within the answer. This could take the form of disadvantages which reduce the size of the benefits to Saltash Toy Box of closing down its retail store, or through a consideration of the extent to which it is likely to be a successful strategy.

Benefits of switching to catalogues/Internet:

• Lower costs/overheads.

• Opportunity for lower prices.

• Greater ability to compete on price with ToysRUs.

• Wider market can be targeted rather than just a small town.

• Increased profit margins.

Drawbacks of switching to catalogues/Internet:

• Will still not be able to compete on price with ToysRUs.

• Will lose its reputation for customer service.

- Loss of USP since children cannot now play with toys before purchase.

- Could lower profits.

- Damage to the brand/loss of local custom.

It is likely that evaluation will be demonstrated by a consideration of the drawbacks of the strategy and the scale of those drawbacks. Some outstanding candidates might consider that the drawbacks may be of a different size over different time periods, therefore it is difficult to judge whether it is likely to be a success.

Level	Descriptor
No mark	Non-rewardable material. No mark is to be awarded if the candidate just re-states the question, i.e. using the Internet will increase the competitiveness of the Saltash Toy Box.
Level 1 1-2 marks	Reference to one effect is given with some weak development or two effects are given with limited or no development of either. If there is just a simple judgement/value attached to one of the effects, 1 mark should be awarded. If this judgement/point has some simple support, the response should be placed at the top of this level.
Level 2 3-5 marks	Reference to two effects is given, with some development of at least one at the lower end. A judgement/point is given at the lower end of the level with some development/support, which includes at least one reason/cause/consequence, etc. At the middle of the level this analysis will be relevant and linked to the judgement/point made. Not simply making more money/profit. Answers at the middle of this level will tend to assume that the judgement/point made will work and that the change of focus will have no downside. At the top of the level there will be some evidence of balance to the point/judgement in the form of advantage/disadvantage, cost/benefit, pro/con or some counterbalancing factor. At the top of the level, candidates will attach some value/importance to one of the effects.
Level 3 6-8 marks	Reference to two effects is given with development of each. A judgement/point is given with some development which includes at least two reasons/causes/consequences, etc. and the use of the 'it depends' rule. Some balance will be given in the form of advantage/disadvantage, pros/cons, costs/benefits. The candidate will be able to show some appreciation that the effects are not 'inevitable' or 'automatic'. At this level, candidates will attach some value/importance to both of the benefits and may make a judgement about which of the effects is more important/valuable to Saltash Toy Box.

Mark schemes for 'Assess' questions (p76)
Indicative content

The aim here is for candidates to consider whether profit is the best measure of business success. The question asks the candidate to 'assess', so the candidate must develop some evidence of balance within the answer. This could take the form of alternative measures of success or through a consideration of the extent to which profit is likely to be a good measure.

Benefits of profit as a measure of success:

- Confirms business strategy is successful as revenue exceeds costs.

- Retained profit can be used for future expansion.

- Comparing profit with that of different businesses is a useful indicator of success.

However, profit is not the only measure of success. It is likely that evaluation will be demonstrated by a consideration of alternative measures of success. These include:

- Revenue.

- Market share.

- Social success – ethical and environmental indicators.

Level	Descriptor
No mark	Non-rewardable material. No mark is to be awarded if the candidate just re-states the question.
Level 1 1-2 marks	Reference to one reason is given with some weak development or two reasons are given with limited or no development of either. If there is just a simple judgement/value attached to one of the reasons, 1 mark should be awarded. If this judgement/point has some simple support, the response should be placed at the top of this level.
Level 2 3-5 marks	Reference to two reasons is given, with some development of at least one at the lower end. A judgement/point is given at the lower end of the level with some development/support, which includes at least one reason/cause/consequence, etc. At the middle of the level this analysis will be relevant and linked to the judgement/point made. Not simply making more money/profit. Answers at the middle of this level will tend to assume that the judgement/point made will work and that the change of focus will have no downside. At the top of the level there will be some evidence of balance to the point/judgement in the form of advantage/disadvantage, cost/benefit, pro/con or some counterbalancing factor. At the top of the level, candidates will attach some value/importance to one of the reasons.
Level 3 6-8 marks	Reference to two reasons is given with development of each. A judgement/point is given with some development which includes at least two reasons/causes/consequences etc. and the use of the 'it depends' rule. Some balance will be given in the form of advantage/disadvantage, pros/cons, costs/benefits. The candidate will be able to show some appreciation that the reasons are not 'inevitable' or 'automatic'. At this level, candidates will attach some value/importance to both of the benefits and may make a judgement about which of the reasons is more important/valuable for different types of business.

Mark schemes for final questions (p82)
Indicative content

The aim here is for candidates to make a judgement as to which element of the marketing mix is likely to improve Megabus' ticket sales. To demonstrate the evaluative skill, candidates could consider the importance of one element of the marketing mix and contrast it with other elements. For instance, they may consider that low prices are essential, and much more important than the quality of the service. Other candidates might highlight the fact that Internet retailing (place) is very important since the cost advantages provided by this allow the price of tickets to be reduced to such low levels. Some candidates might consider time periods and suggest that in the longer term improving the product (service) quality might become more important to Megabus' ticket sales, especially if rival transport providers lower their prices. There is no right or wrong answer to this question, but candidates should aim to make a judgement which is supported. Candidates may consider the following ideas as part of their answer:

Possible reasons why elements of the marketing mix might be important:

- Price – Megabus is seen as a no-frills bus service.

- Product – Without increasing quality, other bus operators might benefit.

- Promotion – Without promotion no one will know about Megabus' low prices.

- Place – online sales enable costs to kept down.

Possible sources of balance:

- Price – it depends on how demand reacts to changes in price and what price it chooses to charge.

- Product – improving quality might increase costs, affecting prices.

- Promotion – is it that important or are low prices the most important factor?

- Place – important, but perhaps secondary to price.

Level	Descriptor
No mark	Non-rewardable material.
Level 1 1-4 marks	One relevant point is identified with some development – there can be a maximum of 4 marks if the links to the point are relevant – one mark per link (up to 3 marks for the links and 1 mark for the relevant point).
	An alternative route to the marks could involve a judgement being given; at the lower end of the level no support will be provided. At the top of the level some support will be given.
	A list of bullet points will gain a maximum of 3 marks, assuming they are all relevant.
Level 2 5-7 marks	Candidates consider the importance of one element of Megabus' marketing mix in allowing the company to improve ticket sales and offer two or more reasons/causes/consequences, etc. in support.

At the lower end of the level no value will be attached to these reasons whilst at the top of the level there will be some recognition of the value of the points made to the business, which may be in the form of offering a counterbalancing point, identifying an advantage and disadvantage, cost/benefit, pro/con, etc.

At the middle of the level a judgement/conclusion will be made but with no support and merely re-states the question.

At the top of the level candidates may offer at least one other factor to balance out the answer. At the top of the level a judgement/conclusion will be made with some support given although not drawn from the analysis and there may be reference to the context.

Level 3 8-10 marks	Candidates consider the importance of an element of the marketing mix which will allow Megabus to increase its sales and offer two or more reasons/causes/consequences, etc. in support.

At the lower end of the level some value will be attached to these reasons whilst at the top of the level there will be clear recognition of the value of the points made to the business, identifying an advantage and disadvantage, cost/benefit, pro/con, etc. or using the 'it depends' rule. At this level candidates are likely to offer at least one other factor (another element of the marketing mix) to balance out the answer.

At the middle of the level a judgement/conclusion will be made with some support drawn from the analysis.

At the top of the level a judgement/conclusion will be clearly drawn from the analysis representing a coherent argument and will refer to the context.

Mark schemes for final questions (p86)
Indicative content

The aim here is for candidates to make a judgement as to how both customers and shareholders might benefit from the growth of Greggs. The evaluative skill will be present through candidates considering the extent to which these stakeholders will gain. Expect candidates to consider the following range of answers:

Consumers (advantages)

- Wider choice of products.

- Cheaper prices due to cost savings being passed on to the customer.

Consumers (disadvantages)

- Loss of individuality of some local products/uniformity.

- Possible increase in prices due to the lack of competition.

Shareholders (advantages)

- A rise in the share price of Greggs.

- Increased profits being made as the company grows.

Shareholders (disadvantages)

- The cost to Greggs of buying Bakers Oven.
- The risk of the company becoming the source of an investigation from the Competition Commission.

Level	Descriptor
No mark	Non-rewardable material.
Level 1 1-3 marks	Answers in this level might be little more than one sentence or a response which has limited development. There will be little or no evidence of any evaluation apart from perhaps a very simplistic judgement with no support offered or limited development. The candidate explains the benefit of the growth of Greggs on only one of the stakeholders identified in the question. A candidate that only explains one benefit cannot go beyond 3 marks. Expect to see no reference to Greggs and answers limited to a generic business. A list of bullet points will get 3 marks maximum, assuming they are all relevant points.
Level 2 4-7 marks	A reasoned response that demonstrates some analysis and evaluation and may have some balance but not as developed as that at Level 3. At the bottom end of this level the candidate will have explained the benefit to both stakeholders using terminology and inter-linkages of ideas. At the lower end of this level the answer might be unbalanced with more being written in support of one option. However, if evaluation is implied or is superficial/weak, e.g. a simple reference is made to which stakeholder is more affected, the maximum mark awardable is 5. At the top end of this level the candidate will have elaborated and developed their evaluation beyond a basic/simple statement and will consider the significance to both customers and shareholders. At the top end of this level, expect to see some balance (with clear reference to Greggs), although any evaluation may still be simplistic in nature. There may be a limited conclusion which is simply a restatement of the question or no conclusion at all. An answer focusing entirely on one style can be awarded full marks in this level provided there is evidence of analysis and evaluation given.
Level 3 8-10 marks	A clear argument is presented which is balanced and refers to the extent to which both customers and shareholders will benefit from the growth of Greggs. This is likely to include at least two factors in support, some balance to show the extent and a rounded conclusion that draws the analysis together. At the very top end a conclusion will be offered that draws on the previous information and is well supported and clearly addresses the command word. Responses will have a clear evaluative slant and will recognise that one stakeholder might benefit more than the other. Expect some candidates to refer to potential drawbacks to customers and shareholders from the growth of Greggs. At the lower end a conclusion might lack development but be an attempt to draw together the analysis offered.